PURE JOY

PURE JOY

Sondra Ray

CELESTIALARTS

BERKELEY, CALIFORNIA

ACKNOWLEDGMENTS

For assistance in the preparation of this book, the author gratefully acknowledges Fredric Lehrman and Mallie Mandel, who proofread the first drafts, and Sandy Asher, who typed the second draft. I thank them all for their time, energy, love, and constant support. And for Ram Dass Giri, who made additional comments on spiritual topics, thank you. And especially for the LRT trainers who contributed chapters; and Laraji, for his words; and R. Coon for his; and most of all to Shastriji, who allowed me to publish his poetry and speeches.

Part of the proceeds of this book will be tithed to the new American Babaji ashram, which will be called "The Center of the Universe Ashram." This ashram will be located at Baca Ranch, Colorado, in the area of the Sangre de Christo Mountains.

I would also like to acknowledge Sheila Singh, Ramloti and Radhe Shyam for their inspiration and devotion to this project. I also acknowledge all those devotees of Babaji who are dedicating their lives to provide us with this ashram for our purification.

If you would like further information or if you would like to make a donation to help develop the ashram, please contact: Radhe Shyam, P.O. Box 95, Crestone, CO 81131 or phone (303) 256-4655.

Quotation by Will Durant from "The Mantrik Power of Sanskrit," by Vasant V. Merchant, Ph.D., Humanities Department, N. Arizona University. *World Union*, Volume XXII, No. 1, January 1982.

CELESTIAL ARTS
P.O. Box 7327
Berkeley, California 94707

Cover design by Ken Scott
Composition by HMS Typography, Inc.

Library of Congress Cataloging-in-Publication Data

Ray, Sondra.
    Pure joy.

    1. Spiritual life.   2. Joy—Religious aspects.
    I. Title.
BL624.R395 1988   291.4'48   86-26911
ISBN 0-89087-491-3

First Printing, 1988

Manufactured in the United States of America

   2   3   4   5   —   92   91   90   89

With deep respect and love
I dedicate this book to:
Sri Trilok Singh (Muniraj)
and
Sri Visnu Datt Shastri (Shastriji)
who constantly show me and the world
the essence of pure joy
and to
all the devotees living and serving
in Babaji's ashrams
across the world. Thank you all.
Om Namaha Shivai.

Dear Babaji,
May everything I write be something beautiful
for God!

—*Sondra Ray*

CONTENTS

FOREWORD

This book could stretch your current reality. In other words, there are a few things in it which may seem unbelievable. Should I leave them out just because of this? No, I don't think so. I don't think you want me to. Should I water them down because they might be easier to swallow? No, I don't think so. I think you want the whole truth. Should I worry that putting out this material will affect my reputation? No, I don't think so. I was asked to explain this now by my teachers, and I am happy to do so. Should I wait until some future date when it might be less of a challenge? No, I don't think so. It is 1988, and it is imperative we all change.

Should I assume you can handle it? *Yes, I Think So.*

It is my job to stick my neck out. Somehow I have ended up with this assignment. If I always worry about what people are going to think, the teachings may not get out. I do acknowledge my publishers for stretching their reality. Mystical things began happening for them because they became willing and open . . . Miracles can happen to you also.

Let's face it. Most people have not been able to maintain PURE JOY most of the time. Because of old frozen ways of thinking, many people are stuck in an old reality that is not working today. Now it is time, and it is possible to go to the reality level that we all deserve to be at. If we want to be really really great, opening to new realities may be required. It was required of me. Now those realities seem normal. Once they did not. I tried not to resist them even though they seemed "different" than before. This helped. It will be easier on you if you can do that also.

Einstein once said, "Great Spirits have always encountered opposition from mediocre minds." Maybe that was true *then*. Maybe it does not have to be true now. I can be a great Spirit *and* so can you be a great Spirit when we remember who we really are. And that is the purpose of this book. I also know that your mind is *not* mediocre . . . just by the mere fact that you are reading this book, I know that. And I know that really there is no such thing as a mediocre mind when one remembers who one is. And again that is the purpose of this book: to remind us that we are *not* mediocre. We are made of the substance of Pure Joy—and we can have that experience always.

Babaji and Jesus are Great Spirits who never forget that is who they are. That is why I feel it is important to use them as an example. They are our inspiration. They came to remind us who we are. The difference is that they do not have doubt. We often do. That is why we need to read a book occasionally to get out of doubt and remember how to feel Pure Joy. We may have to do a purification technique to get back to the joy. The great news is that doing this is joyful in itself and fun. Reading this book could even be blissful.

It is a joy for me to share this with you.

All my love,

—*Sondra Ray*

SONDRA'S PRAYERS BEFORE THIS BOOK

I am here with you, God,
I give you my body
I give you my mind
I give you my voice
I give you my arms and hands
I give you my feet
I give you my spine
I give you my heart
I give you my lungs
I give you my cells
    and all my organs
I give you my life
I give you my relationships
I give you the Loving Relationships Training
    and all my books
—and everything else!

Dear God,
I want to be sharper,
I want to be better
I want to be more alive . . .
    More forgiving
    More loving
    More understanding

I want to let go faster

INTRODUCTION

We all want to experience the joy and wonder of life. Sometimes we do, yet at other times we wonder why we cannot. We may vaguely remember Bible verses which imply that we can have joy, such as John 15:11, "These things I have spoken to you, that my joy may be in you, that your joy may be full." We may have been told that joy is our natural state. But we cannot help but wonder, then, why aren't we in touch with joy more often?

Some people say that joy is the highest expression of God that there is. For me, joy had always been associated with a feeling of celebration, as well as a gratitude for the infinite beauty of life. I noticed that whenever I felt clear and had wonderful, positive thoughts, not only did I feel joy, I felt like sharing that joy with others. And, obviously then, whenever I was unclear or had dark, negative thoughts, the joy all seemed to disappear.

But I began to wonder—did the joy really disappear, or had I just suppressed it somehow? Was it somehow possible to recapture the simple joy I had known as a child?

I remembered that childhood joy so clearly—the joy I had felt at age six, before I started school and before my father had become ill. Back then I had always felt on top of the world, always in ecstasy. I loved everyone, and I showed it. I cared about everything, was interested in everything. I was always in awe of life. My long, spiraling red curls and freckles may have made me appealing, but it was what I felt inside that really mattered. People seemed to love to have me around. I would visit the aged and the poor in my town, roaming around and spreading joy.

It was easy, because I *felt* it. It was *real*!

But what happened? When did that joy leave me? When did I stop feeling like that? Well, for one thing, my father became ill. I watched his slow death, and my own joy seemed to die. After my father died, I spent twenty years recovering. School was another thing—I became a serious student and became involved in everyone's problems. When I grew up I got married, and later divorced—and spent twelve years recovering from *that*.

What happened to the joy? As I pondered this question, thinking back over my childhood and young adulthood, I became increasingly concerned that the essence of that joy simply *had* to be recoverable. If all things are possible, I said to myself, then it must be possible to return to joy.

I decided to do some research, travelling throughout the world, reading everything I could, talking to great spiritual teachers. I began to study techniques of purification, mostly from religious traditions. I analyzed which method seemed the fastest route to that feeling of joy for myself, as well as which were the most enjoyable. I also found that when I used these purification techniques to cleanse myself of unwanted negativity, confusion, and suppressed emotion, the joy just came right out of me, bubbling up like a great natural spring.

And so, using the techniques I discovered in my travels and studies— the techniques that are now presented as this book—I found the joy in life again. The joy returned. It had never really *gone* anywhere; it had just been buried deep within myself, beneath layers of negative thoughts and fears. My ego, I discovered, had been in the way.

The techniques of spiritual purification discussed in this book come from many different places and experiences. What is written here is a synthesis of many inspirational traditions. Some of these insights came about as a result of my personal adventures in the far East and others as a direct result of using these techniques or of developing them from inspirational reading, especially reading from A *Course in Miracles*.

I wrote this book to ensure my own return to Pure Joy and to share what I have learned—and to inspire others to do the same. Ironically, just as I was writing this Introduction, a man called me on the phone, and when I told him that I was writing the introduction to my book titled *Pure Joy*, he said, "My dear, it is the purity that counts."

Mother Teresa has said that the problem with the world is "spiritual deprivation." Yes, if we were all spiritually nourished, things would be very different. Try to imagine a world where everyone acknowledged oneness with God and their own joy with their own thoughts. Try to imagine a world where everyone took responsibility for their actions, where everyone knew that what they do comes from what they think. Imagine that everyone guarded their thoughts carefully and nourished only high, loving positive thoughts that produced positive results. Imagine that everyone spent their time doing what gladdened them—what kept them pure. And if they faltered, they would help each other get back on track quickly. Imagine a world in which everyone was moving in the direction of more aliveness and more joy.

Imagine a world with rapid techniques for staying clear and ways of expressing love to God that were fun and wonderful to do, where people did ceremonies and rituals together that made them feel ecstatic, where everyone was in a healed body and in a Holy Relationship, where there was music and celebration everywhere.

These are some of the goals we have in the Loving Relationships Training Family, which we call "OHANA" (Ohana is a Hawaiian word which means, literally, "an extended family of people who breathe together"). Is this an unrealistic utopia we envision? Perhaps not. Perhaps if we start now, all of us together, others will come and help us. Perhaps you will join us in bringing joy and peace to the world. We welcome you in the Ohana. We look forward to playing with you and working with you. We welcome your love and ideas.

In this book I share with you some of the writings of members of the Loving Relationships Training Ohana. These people are trainers in the Loving Relationships Training, and it is a potent offering to have their writings about God and about pure joy included here.

The Kingdom of God—which is *Joy*—is all of us, together.

WHAT IS GOD?

What is God? God is unlimited, and, therefore, beyond definition. God's own answer to this question was "I am that I am."

What does that mean? It means that "I am unlimited potential." That would be the only answer that God could give.

Some will try to explain that God is "creative principle," "embodiment of all substance," "intelligence," "love," and "power," "containing all things." Others talk about the seven main aspects of God (from the Church of Religious Science): (1) *God is Principle* (for example, perfect harmony; God does not change); (2) *God is Truth* (to know the truth about any condition heals it); (3) *God is Life* (joy is the highest expression); (4) *God is Love* (when you love God more than your problem, you will be healed); (5) *God is Intelligence* (all things are possible); (6) *God is Soul* (that aspect in which God is able to individualize Himself); and (7) *God is Spirit* (spirit is that which cannot be destroyed).

More important than any attempt at definition, however, is realizing that your life/your power/your health/and your happiness depend on your acceptance of God and that you and God are one. When you identify yourself with the truth of your being, life can never again be disappointing or unproductive. God will be revealed to you to the degree that you acknowledge the spirit in all people and in *all* things.

In other words, your spiritual self must come forth, and you must see the spiritual self in everyone and in everything.

WHAT IS JOY?

It has been said that joy is the highest expression of God that there is. If we wish for joy in our lives, we must remember that we were made in the image of God and we *are* God-like. This book will help you to remember who you are and will support you in joyfully loving your God-self and God more.

When you are feeling great, and everything is working well, and you are getting everything you want, it is easy to feel joy and to love God. But when you don't feel well, and things are not going so great, and you are not getting what you want, then it seems very difficult to love God and find joy.

And yet, *loving God IS pure joy.*

If you could remember to love God at those times when you are low, then you would be uplifted, heal yourself, and things *would* start working.

The suggestions given in this book are those that we as trainers of the Loving Relationships Training use regularly in our lives. The more we do them, the more joy we experience. We have tried to make them a constant—a way of life—not something we do just now and then when we need a high. We try to *live* this way, practicing these methods of loving God regularly.

We invite you to join us.

CHAPTER 1

HOW TO LOVE GOD

Service

The formula for happiness and joy that my teacher Babaji gave is LOVE, TRUTH, SIMPLICITY, AND SERVICE TO MANKIND. Service to mankind has several parts: firstly, your work should be a form of your worship. This is what He called "karma yoga" or work dedicated to God. If you dedicate all your work to God and the service of humanity, you will have a new experience of working. Look and see if it is that right now. If it isn't, try to improve your present working situation so that it becomes more of a service. Or if you can't seem to do this, maybe it would be appropriate to create a new job that fulfills this purpose. Of course, we recommend that you have a job that is pleasurable to you, as sharing that pleasure is naturally a service.

The second part is seeing other ways that you could serve humanity beyond your job. This could mean joining service and humanitarian organizations that improve the planet and people's lives or serving some individual or group that you respect. If there is someone you consider to be a master, for example, someone who is really making a contribution to the planet, think about offering your services free to that person. You can get very high doing this and it will contribute to your joy. Having been a waitress, a nurse, and a Virgo by birth, this was quite natural to me. I was trained to pay attention to service all the time. As I began to study enlightenment, I found that there were many wonderful people I could serve in that field. I tried to do it selflessly, for the sheer joy of giving and pleasure of learning. Now many serve me and I have never had to ask them to do it. The Universe gave it back.

If you respect a group that contributes to your spiritual growth and/or you like how a group is contributing to mankind, consider being a volunteer. All you have to do to get started is ask "How can I serve you? . . . I have this amount of time per week."

Try it.

At the ashrams in India, there is a time each day for "karma yoga" where you serve the area by cleaning and beautifying everything. This could include gardening/carrying rocks/building latrines/cleaning latrines/carrying wood/building bridges, temples, dorms, etc. You would be surprised how much devotees get out of this manual labor. How about it? What can you do now to beautify your neighborhood and your town?

What can you do to help the poor and the hungry?

What can you do to help the sick?

The third part is to have an attitude of service at all times. Rather than wait around for your allotted service times, why not always be thinking in that mode? How can you serve people and places around you in each moment? How can you make this moment better for yourself and everyone? How can you raise the quality of thoughts that are going on in your space now? How can you cheer people up/clean things up/make things better? How can you serve God at all times? Think about it!

Think for a moment of a person who helped you, a person who shared a seminar or a healer who made you feel better, about something that turned your life around. And then take a minute to appreciate the help and movement you got.

Finally, take time to experience the gratitude you have for that person. You might want to call and/or write and express your thanks. People will appreciate *you* for sharing what you know that might help them. When something is good and works, tell others. Help them overcome their fear of change and their fear of trying new things. Do not push them, but become an inspiration. Every chance you get, tell others what has worked for you in the arena of spiritual enlightenment. Withholding is not your function. Withholding is of the ego.

Love is extension. "To withhold the smallest gift is not to know love's purpose." *A Course in Miracles* says that "love offers everything, forever . . ." "Specialness not only sets apart, but serves as grounds from which attack on those who seem 'beneath' the special one is 'natural.' Specialness is a great dictator of the wrong decisions." (P. 465, *A Course in Miracles* [CIM].

> *Would it be possible for you to hate your brother if you were like him? Can you attack him if you realized you journey with him, to a goal that is just the same? Your brother is your friend because his Father created him like you. There is no difference. You have been given to each other that love might be extended, not cut off from each other. What you keep is lost to you. (P. 466, [CIM])*

What you give away you can have . . . enroll your brother. Bring him to God with you!

Worship

To worship is to reverence the *worth* of something or someone. In the book *Being A CHRIST* by Anne and Peter Meyer, it is explained that "worship" stems from the root "wor," which is also found in the words "work" and "worth." Jesus said, "My Father works, and I work even now." Babaji repeatedly stated that KARMA YOGA, or "work dedicated to God," is one of the most important things for purification, for achieving happiness and joy. He said, "Work is Worship." You may not have considered that before. Consider it now! Dedicate all of your work to God as a form of worship and see what happens!

The Meyers go on to say that:

> *Worship is the highest, most non-judging form of love. If we worship a person, we see no wrong in him whatsoever. We open ourselves completely to him and become his willing servant. If we worship our teacher, we will learn very quickly*

3

*and completely from him, for we will be open and receptive
to all he has to say.*

*Worship, however, is invalid unless we worship ALL OF
LIFE, for equality is the only Truth.*

By worshipping you will gain the most out of life. By worshipping
you will feel the best you can feel. By worshipping you will contribute to a more advanced civilization. Worship is natural. Not to worship is unnatural.

There are many religious ceremonies that are forms of worship.
Chanting is a form of worship. It is also a purification and I discuss
this in depth in the following section. The highest form of prayer,
i.e. gratitude, is a form of worship. Everyone knows singing hymns
that are uplifting is a good form of worship. Next I give two examples of worship: The Altar and Spiritual Poetry.

The Altar

One wonderful way to love God is to prepare one of more altars in
your home. I learned this in Bali when I was working on the God
Training (LRT Spiritual Retreat) and while writing the book *Drinking the Divine*. I was simply amazed to find that every single home
had an altar. Not only that, but every single home had a temple, and
they actually *used* these altars and temples daily!

They wouldn't consider starting the workday without doing daily
prayer rituals and ceremonies. Every morning the family members
prepare elaborate flower and fruit decorations, and they use a lot of
incense. These preparations are placed on the altar along with the
prayers. Then, and only then, do they begin their work—which is
all dedicated to God.

The Balinese people were a great inspiration to me. The first thing
I did when I went home was to prepare a temple room. This was
very pleasurable. I found a beautiful antique rosewood table with
Roman columns that I chose for the altar. I asked a friend of mine
to do a large glass etching of my favorite picture of my teacher
Babaji standing on a mountain with robes blowing. This came out

4

beautifully, and I placed it over the altar. Then, on the altar itself, I put pictures of Jesus, Saibaba, and my other teachers. I placed flowers, candles, and incense holders. I put out all the mala beads I had collected in India and other appropriate holy objects. I must say that this altar has produced a lot of joy and respect in my heart. It is the first thing that I see when I enter my flat. On Christmas Eve of this year, I set up another altar in my bedroom and stayed up all night and meditated near it. Now I have an altar in every room.

You might have resistance to an altar if you have not cleared your feelings about religion and any disappointment you have around that subject. To do that I recommend that you go back to your original church and sit in a pew and breathe a lot. Forgive everything that was confusing and be grateful for everything that was good and inspiring and loving.

It does not matter what religion you were or were not raised in. What matters is a reverence and love for God *now*. An altar will help you achieve this reverence, this respect. It will remind you to think holy thoughts and perhaps inspire you to do spiritual purification. It will remind you of your love for God and your absolute connection. When people come to your home they, too, will be inspired, and they will not only treat you with more respect, they will begin to think of their own spiritual life. They will appreciate you for reminding them that they, too, love God—but may be forgetting to express it.

One of my favorite types of incense, by the way, is Blue Pearl from Muktananda's ashram. This can be obtained at metaphysical book stores or else at Muktananda Centers (Sidda Yoga Foundations).

Sometimes, when I have a problem that seems difficult, I write Babaji and Jesus a letter. I absolutely bare my soul to them. Then I place this letter on my altar. Help and solutions come rapidly. It has never failed yet.

Try kneeling in front of your altar and see how you feel about that. Do you resist it? Do you feel embarrassed and silly? What do you feel? This simple ritual actually does help you to feel humble. It helps you to let go.

Now try lying face down, spreading out all the way in front of your altar. This usually stirs up a lot of feelings and is, for me, an even quicker way to let go. If your mind needs to be "snapped," this could possibly do it for you. Chances are it will really open your heart.

Reading Spiritual Poetry: The Divine Mother

Have you ever considered the possible JOY of indulging in spiritual poetry? It is one way to honor and praise God. It can also be purifying for your consciousness. Perhaps you may even begin to write poetry yourself!

I could give you many examples of this kind of beautiful writing; however, I am going to single out the poet Shastriji, since I am dedicating this book to him. You can read all about Shastriji in Part V of this book, where you will also see a picture of him and be able to read his speeches.

I want to give a few samples here of his verses because they are an excellent example of worship. These verses are taken form his book *HAIDAKHANDI SAPTA SATI: Seven Hundred Verses In Praise Of The Divine Mother Of Haidakhan.* I thank him for permission to publish this. I had so much pleasure reading this book that I asked him if I could put my favorite verses on tape. He agreed and this tape is now available.

Shastriji is one my supreme teachers about pure joy. He always seems to be in a state of bliss. He is everything you can imagine a Saint to be. Being with him *is* Pure Joy. Shastriji is a high Priest, he is an Ayurvedic doctor, a gifted Clairvoyant and the mouthpiece of Babaji (for information on Babaji, the Immortal Avatar, see Part V).

Shastriji is, according to Babaji, one of the most learned men on earth (and one of the purest). Babaji once said that Shastriji has been a poet in all life times. To me, reading his words stimulates Joy . . .

SOME VERSES IN PRAISE OF THE DIVINE MOTHER Reading these verses out loud will put you into pure joy.

> *Oh, Sivai, You are the embodiment of ultimate bliss and conscious Energy. You are supreme knowledge of the Absolute. You are the image of infinite compassion, unfathomable as*

*is the deep sea. Oh Durga, Goddess of the universe, I pros-
trate before you.*

*Oh Universal Mother, you give me shelter. In truth, You are
the one who gives life to all the beings of this world. You are
the physician who curses the fever of the life and death cycles
of this wheel of life. You are the source of life and liberation
to all living beings. We pray to that timeless Energy which
resides as mother Goddess in Haidakhan. Remembering You
is to crown this life with success, to attain liberation.*

*Oh Mother, the divine beauty of Your forms is beyond all
words. You alone take care that this child of yours safely crosses
the sea of life. Oh Durga, you reside within the lotus-heart
of Eternal Lord Siva, the Supreme Master. Oh, Durga,
destroyer of sins, I bow to you.*

*You are the embodiment of divine speech and hidden supreme
knowledge. You reside in the temple of Lord Siva's heart. The
prayers of the Vedas are directed to Your divinity. You are the
embodiment of the initial see of "Om" and are rooted therein.
You are the Energy of kundalini, giving birth to creation. The
knowledge of You in this divine form enables the yogis no more
to return to the mother's womb.*

*You are adorned with a face that is luminous like the full
moon. Your smile is tender and Your forehead is like a flaw-
less mirror that reflects and issues divine light. It is said that
he who meditates on the divine form of Her whose face shines
like the full moon attains all happiness.*

*You are of sublime beauty with Your luminous eyes. Your face
is of incomparable beauty, radiant with spontaneous JOY and
Your smiling lips of crimson color. The whole of Your appearance has the softness of a budding orange blossom.*

*Oh, Goddess, who upholds the universe, You give perfection
to all beings. You are the Beloved of Lord Naryana. To those
who take refuge in You, You grant the most precious boons
and give them happiness. Mother, we prostrate before You.*

Your Energy is beyond the power even of Brahma, Visnu and Mahesvara. Your form is eternal everlasting Peace. You are the ultimate root of all of the elements. Oh Mother, You are mistress of the quality of goodness and of all other qualities. It is to You that the trinity of Brahman, Visnu and Siva address their prayers. Great Mother, to You we bow.

Praying to You with Vedic Mantras, Your annihilate the fear of those beings of the world whom You protect, giving them their desired boons and all divine perfection. To You, Oh Mother, we bow.

Music as a form of worship goes without saying. It is obvious. But have you really made it a regular habit to listen to the right music?

The music I myself like to listen to is mostly sacred chants I have collected from all of my travels. I also like classical music and new age music. I have any one of these playing every day as a way of worshipping and purifying myself. I am currently doing a little study on which of my tapes produce the most healing effect on the body and which of my tapes inspire a respectful attitude of worship along with joy.

One tape that is most joyful and in the category of Praise that I recommend is *ALLELUIA BY RAFAEL*—an extremely interesting and exciting new age musician.

CHAPTER 2
PURIFYING YOURSELF

MIRACLES ARE EVERYONE'S RIGHT . . .
BUT PURIFICATION IS NECESSARY FIRST.
—A Course In Miracles, *Chapter 1, page 1*

Chanting

Chanting is a type of singing that is both a form of praise and a form of purification. However, I am going to emphasize the purification aspect of it, since the aspect of praise is more obvious.

Chanting a mantra is one of the most powerful things you could do for yourself. A mantra is a sacred syllable, word, or set of words, which, through constant repetition and reflection upon, helps one attain perfection and God realization. "Japa" is a word used in the East to describe the act of repeating the mantra or repeating God's name.

The mantra *OM NAMAHA SHIVAI* is the main mantra chanted at the Babaji ashrams. My teacher, Babaji, told us all, of all faiths, to "always repeat God's name whatever you do, wherever you are, repeat the name of the Lord." He said *OM NAMAHA SHIVAI* is the original mantra. (Sanskrit is the original language and it is more powerful to chant in that language.) Babaji told us that *OM NAMAHA SHIVAI* is the highest thought that there is.

Its literal translation is: "Oh, Lord Shiva, I bow to thee in reverence." (*Shiva* is that part of God that burns or destroys our ignorance.)

9

This mantra has many meanings; for example, it also means: "Infinite Spirit, Infinite Being, and Infinite Manifestation." Therefore, chanting it helps you to manifest the infinite at the same time you are burning out your resistance and ego. It also means, "Oh, Lord, you are my refuge, thy will be done," and, "I bow to the God within."

The mantra is like nectar, nourishing you. It is like plugging yourself into the Source. It charges you up. It leads to remembering your total union with God. It enlivens the inner consciousness and helps us overcome suffering. It provides protection and brings inner peace.

Behold the glory and the power of the Divine Name! The Divine Name, or mantra, IS divinity. God's Name is the greatest treasure on earth. The chanting of God's Name or mantra is one of the best forms of devotion there is. Repetition of the mantra purifies the heart. You can achieve all things through japa. Japa yoga is the easiest, quickest, safest, surest and cheapest way of attaining God Realization. Take refuge in His name. All troubles, miseries, pains and sorrows will come to an end. The Divine Name burns out all your karma and errors. The Name of God is the master-key for success in life and God-realization. God's name, or the mantra, is the foundation of spirituality.

The name of God is also a cure for all disease. (This is called Divine Namapathy.) You can take this medicine (repeating God's Name) for curing anything; and you can administer this medicine to others, by sitting at the side of the patient and singing God's Name with sincere devotion and faith. The only real Doctor is God.

There was a case reported where doctors had pronounced the son of a landlord as dying—the case was absolutely hopeless. Devotees took the case into their hands. They did continuous *Kirtan* day and night for seven days around the bed of the patient. Kirtans are devotional songs containing the name or aspect of the deity worshipped (Lord Shiva, The Divine Mother, Vishnu, etc.). These are to be repeated as many times as one wants to. The patient stood up on the seventh day and began to sing God's Name for himself. He had recovered completely.

The mantra is obviously also a supreme "pick me up" in case you are going into gloom, despair, or low energy. Release *does* happen!

By singing *OM NAMAHA SHIVAI*, God's grace is evoked.

To have an experience of the all-encompassing, deeper meanings of *OM NAMAHA SHIVAI*, read the following stanzas (perhaps out loud) from the tape, *OM NAMAHA SHIVAI*, by Laraji. You will have a special experience just reading these words. Listening to and chanting with Laraji's tape is even better.

Om Namaha Shivai

Peace all over the existing Creation, by virtue of the fact
That its Creator is present as Omni-Present Perfection

Be still and feel this everlasting source of beauty.
This everlasting source of Peace
This everlasting Source of Freedom
Om Namaha Shivai . . . Om Shanti

Be still and touch this fundamental sense of oneness
This fundamental sense of now
This fundamental sense of Power
Om Namaha Shivai . . . Om Shanti

Be still and know this Everpresent sense of freedom
This everpresent sense of light
This everpresent sense of I AM . . . now here with you.
Om Namaha Shivai . . . Om Shanti

Be still and feel this underlying sense of Oneness.
This underlying sense of now
This underlying sense of beauty
This underlying sense of WOW
Om Namaha Shivai . . . Om Shanti

Be still and know this fundamental sense of feeling
This fundamental sense of here
This fundamental sense of oneness
This fundamental sense of clear
Om Namaha Shivai . . . Om Shanti

Be still and know this everlasting sense of oneness
This everlasting sense of safety
This everlasting sense of order
Om Namaha Shivai . . . Om Shanti

Be still and know this fundamental sense of purpose
This fundamental sense of here
This fundamental sense of reason
This fundamental felt so clear
Om Namaha Shivai . . . Om Shanti

Be still and touch this everlasting sense of presence
This everlasting sense of here
This everlasting sense of union
This everlasting self so clear
Om Namaha Shivai . . . Om Shanti

Be still and feel this fundamental sense of reverence
This fundamental sense of wealth
This fundamental sense of prosperity
This fundamental sense of here and now
Om Namaha Shivai . . . Om Shanti

Be still and feel this everlasting sense of self
This fundamental sense of "I"
Thus all-pervading sense of now
This everlasting sense of here
Om Namaha Shivai . . . Om Shanti

Be still and feel this fundamental sense of oneness
This fundamental sense of Union
This fundamental sense of now . . . here . . . this
Om Namaha Shivai . . . Om Shanti

Be still and feel this underlying frame of reverence
This underlying frame of power
This underlying frame of self . . . SUPREME
Be still and feel this everlasting sense of oneness
This everlasting sense of harmony

This everlasting sense of purpose
Om Namaha Shivai . . . Om Shanti

Be still and know this everlasting sense of tranquility
This everlasting sense of peace
This everlasting sense of harmony
Now . . . This Way . . .
Om Namaha Shivai . . . Om Shanti

Be still and feel this fundamental sense of here
This all pervading sense of now
This everlasting sense of self
Om Namaha Shivai . . . Om Shanti

Be still and feel that underlying sense of presence
That underlying sense of substance
That underlying sense of power . . . DIVINE
Om Namaha Shivai . . . Om Shanti

Be still and touch this all pervading sense of Universe
This all pervading sense of now
This all pervading sense of homeland
This all pervading sense of here
Om Namaha Shivai . . . Om Shanti

Be still and touch this all pervading sense of self
This all pervading sense of power
This all pervading sense of perfection
This all pervading sense of now
Om Namaha Shivai . . . Om Shanti

Be and Know
  Feel
    Sense
      Touch
        Receive
          Return
Om Namaha Shivai . . . Om Shanti

Be still and know
Be still and feel
Be still and know
Be still

Just listening to the name *Om Namaha Shivai* being chanted, you will experience delight and healing.

Singing devotional songs is a wonderful way of inspiring joy. We have collected songs sung at Babaji's ashrams, in both book and tape form. The collection consists of Kirtans and Bhajans. Bhajans are religious hymns, telling a brief story. The Lord is given praise in all His glory, in His many forms and manifestations. The underlying theme is one of joy, gratitude and love.

Babaji said that "Kirtan should come to you naturally, through your soul . . . You should sing devotional music in a way that stirs the heart, in harmony and in slow rhythm. Whenever you make music, singing or playing it should leave a memory in the mind."

The following is an example of a beautiful song from "Haidakhan Bhajans." This is called *Prabhuji*. I will give the English translation:

Beloved Lord those who sing your praises
Are exceptional people.
Those who give their lives for your name's sake
Are Exceptional People

Having made me drink the nectar of your love
Make me now your great devotee (one who wants only you)
The one who pours the nectar into the cup
Is exceptional
The Cup, too, is exceptional
Beloved Lord . . .

In case you are one of those people who may resist anything that seems "foreign" or anything like "Eastern philosophy" or "Hindu Mysticism" or anything that seems to you almost "anti-American" in tone—let me suggest the following: Stay open. Be willing to see things differently. Be willing to see something that is "different" differently.

14

Try to look at what works. I don't even bother writing about what doesn't work. I am interested in results, purification, enlightenment, joy, and anything God-like. I only share what will bring you joy.

Recently I received a wonderful letter from a student/friend who shared with me what she had to go through in accepting chanting, Babaji, and Indian philosophy. Her letter makes some very very important points:

> *It was very liberating for me to share with you the chanting of Babaji's ashram in Hawaii. Up until then I had resisted Indian religion. I thought it foreign and alien and that religion was something one gets from one's own culture. I thought that to adopt the Hindu practices, or whatever, was to deny my own heritage and try to be something I am not. Well, that made a lot of sense to me and served me well enough, until I experienced the chanting of the Arti with you in Hawaii. All of my resistance left me and I felt the effects of the chanting in my body almost instantly. !!What A JOY!!!!!*
>
> *Now I realize that these practices are very ancient and universal; and so refined that any human being can tap into them and experience enlightenment. It was a VERY empowering experience for me. I felt moved deeply and as if parts of myself deep inside of me were waking from their dormant state and finding a voice, a form of expression. I am grateful to you for introducing me to these things and grateful to myself for trusting enough to allow this into my life.*
>
> *—Love, Martha McKay*

Aarati is that portion of the Hindu worship service in which lights (usually in the form of wicks burning ghee or purified butter) are waved before an image of God, as a symbol of light overcoming the darkness of human ignorance. To offer *aarati* is to praise the name of the Divine as prayers. The prayers appeal to His grace for the fulfillment of all desires and to seek refuge. *Aarati* is an offering of the inner self to the Divine.

Every time you sing the *Aartari* you are blessed with Babaji's energy. Here is an example of some verses (translated into English):

Holy master show grace to me
Show grace to me, have mercy on me
O Lord Thou art brother of the humble and giver of all
Show grace to me, have mercy on me

Thou art the trinity—the embodiment of knowledge
  the knower and the object of knowledge
Show grace to me, have mercy on me
Thou holy divine master of eternal form—
EMBODIMENT OF JOY
Show grace to me, have mercy on me.

Meditation

Meditation cannot be done by thinking. Nor does meditation mean making your mind go blank. It is not a kind of hypnosis or suggestibility. It has nothing to do with the occult either.

Meditation might be called a systematic technique for concentrating and taking hold of our latent mental power. It might simply be a method for jumping into the unconscious. It does consist of training the mind so that you can go from the surface level of consciousness into the very depths.

But to jump there without thinking, a device is needed. This device will push you to the unknown. The device is an artificial trick to put your rational mind at ease. Sufis used dance as a technique. Zen teachers used Koans (puzzles). Rajneesh used a vigorous method called Chaotic Meditation with catharsis.

Maharishi uses a personal mantra that you are given by an instructor which you say silently to yourself. This is called Transcendental Meditation (TM). It is the type of meditation I was taught. It seemed most in harmony with Rebirthing and Chanting. Fortunately we now have an LRT trainer who was a teacher of TM and was with Maharishi for 15 years, Vincent Betar. He has written about this in Part IV. Maharishi also teaches Physical Immortality. He has actually scientifically, statistically proven that TM produces rejuvenation and longevity and youthing. It is a scientifically proven process to stop aging. If you are interested in further information, call your nearest TM center.

You can also make up our own "music meditations" and study the results on yourself.

In his book *Practical Spirituality,* John Randolph Price defines meditation as:

> . . . *a relaxing of the body, a stilling of the emotions, and a narrowing of attention so that the mind may contemplate the inner reality and move into another dimension in consciousness. It is a gentle raising of vibrations so that one may come into alignment with the spiritual self.*

He goes on to mention the benefits of meditation, which medical and academic studies have released evidence to support:

> *Meditation will alleviate stress,*
> *Reduce high blood pressure,*
> *Increase resistance to disease.*
> *Increase the autonomic stability of the nervous system,*
> *Improve the power of concentration,*
> *Tap deep reserves of intelligence,*
> *Contribute to mental clarity,*
> *Stabilize emotions,*
> *Improve human relations,*
> *Relieve insomnia,*
> *Improve coordination of mind and body,*
> *Increase learning ability*
>   *and*
> *Boost creativity.*

And finally, he states:

> *But of even greater importance are the spiritual benefits; the objective must be to establish a channel resulting in an outpouring of the higher energy of Spirit.*

The Highest Thought and Gratitude

In all of my books, I have defined enlightenment as being certain that your thoughts produce your results and taking responsibility for raising the quality of your thoughts. Let's take a look at what *A Course in Miracles* says about creating your own reality:

17

You may believe that you are responsible for what you do, but not for what you think. The truth is that you are responsible for what you think because it is only at this level that you can exercise choice. What you do comes from what you think (p. 25, CIM, Text).

As a man thinketh, so does he perceive. Therefore seek not to change the world, but choose to change your mind about the world . . . (p. 415, CIM, Text).

It is impossible that the Son of God be merely driven by events outside of Him. It is impossible that happenings that came to Him were not His choice. His power of decision is the determining factor of every situation in which he seems to find Himself, by choice or accident (p. 418, CIM, Text).

What you desire you will see . . . you made the world you see.

The *Course* is always asking why you condone insane negative thinking? In the next moment, you can experience Heaven or Hell, depending on which thought you choose to think. You always have free choice to go toward the Spirit (positive thinking) or the ego (negative thinking). Bliss is only one thought away, and that thought is up to you. If you return all your thinking to the Holy Spirit you will be in joy. Say only this, but mean it:

> *I AM responsible for what I see.*
> *I choose the feelings I experience, and I*
> *decide upon the goal I would achieve.*
> *And everything that seems to happen to me*
> *I ask for, and receive as I have asked.*
> *(p. 418, CIM, Text.)*

Deceive yourself no longer that you are helpless in the face of what is done to you.

What are the highest thoughts you can think?

Gratitude is something to think about as much as possible. I remember one of my teachers saying that when you get to the point where you have real gratitude for even the sidewalk you are walking upon, then you are getting somewhere. You may think you have gratitude for people, but *how deep* is it? Is it just a fleeting moment's worth, or do you really feel it and experience it? I don't think I was ever able to know what real gratitude could be like until I was able to lie on my bed and sob over my deep feelings of love and appreciation for someone. (Recently, I experienced this for the LRT staff.) This lasted for quite some time and I said, "Oh, this is real gratitude." Then I gave thanks to God, but I felt humble. How was I able to arrive at that moment? By continually clearing myself so that my heart became more and more open to feeling gratitude at a much deeper level. Now this often happens spontaneously.

You may feel gratitude, *but* do you express it? Do you express it directly to those you feel it for? If not, why not?

Do you thank God for what you have? What you are grateful for increases. Find ways to express gratitude to God. This will bring you joy.

Example of High Thoughts for Night Time Programming Fear thoughts, pain thoughts, and grief thoughts create the ugliness called old age. Joyous thoughts, love thoughts, and ideal thoughts create the beauty called youth. Practice acquiring the consciousness of childhood. Visualize the Divine Child within.

> *I now realize that there is within me a spiritual joy-body ever young, ever beautiful. I have beautiful, spiritual mind, eyes, nose, mouth, skin—the body of the Divine Infant, which now, tonight, is perfect. Well, dear _____(your name)_____, there is a divine alchemist within. The divine alchemist is within my temple, constantly coining new and beautiful baby cells. The spirit of youth is within my temple—this human form divine, and all is well. Om Santi! Santi! Santi! (Peace! Peace! Peace!) I think a happy thought for all the world. May all the world be happy and blest. Within me there is a perfect form—the form Divine. I am now all that I desire to be! I visualize daily my beautiful being until I breathe it into expression! I am a Divine Child, all my needs are being now and forever supplied! Infinite Love fills my mind and thrills my body with its perfect life.*

> *From:* Life & Teaching of the Masters of the Far East, Volume I, *by Baird T. Spalding.*

Spiritual Books

Why not make a pact with yourself to read only enlightened books for a while? By this I mean why not read only books where the author understands that thoughts are creative and results come from those thoughts? These books are not only spiritually uplifting, they are also able to accelerate your process and help you stay high.

Naturally, I hope you will be inspired to read all the books I have written and those by Bob Mandel, director of the Loving Relationship Training. There are many other books that we recommend and sell in our trainings that support our work and produce great results.

We encourage our students to take a year to read nothing but enlightened books, and we tell them to see what happens. Everyone who has actually done this assignment has thanked us immensely for the recommendation. That is what each of us who are now partners for the LRT did when we started this work years ago. We attribute our leadership role to many factors; however, reading spiritual literature as a form of purification is definitely one thing we would all acknowledge and we are very grateful for.

I remember when I began reading the *Life and Teachings of the Masters of the Far East*, a five volume set of powerful books. I read the first volume and was so shocked and stunned and excited that I could not tolerate reading the other four volumes until a year later.

The book I am going to single out here is *A Course in Miracles*. After you read the following, you will see why.

A Course in Miracles

What would you do if you knew there was someone who knew all the answers to all problems; someone who had mastered life completely; someone who would put you into instant joy, someone who could heal you, someone who had even conquered death? Would you go see him? Would you at least consider seeking him out? Probably you would, right?

What would you do if you knew Jesus was still around and you could find Him? Would you go find Him? Would you check Him out, even if you were not raised a Christian? Yes, probably you would.

What would you do if you knew there was a book written by Him in the last decade, a book written by Him for modern times? A book that cleared up all the confusion in the Bible, and all the confusion you might have had in religion, a book that explained everything, answered all questions and taught you how to heal yourself completely, and a book that taught you how to have perfect relationships? Would you read it? What if this book itself was a miracle? Would you read it? Maybe you would. You might consider it, right?

That book is here. Jesus is here through it. The answers *are* in it. That book is *A Course in Miracles*. It is available now. You can have the answers now. You can be healed now. You can receive salvation now. Your life can work now.

Personally, I feel that it is important to learn from someone who has mastered what we are trying to learn. The problem with learning from someone like Jesus is that one has to confront all one's feelings on the subject of Jesus and religion—not an easy topic, because of all the confusion about religion and religious wars.

Do you know that the foundation of Christianity was actually written down about 30 *years* after Jesus' death and that much of it was written in a way that can easily be misinterpreted, since it was written through the ego? The ego is based on the thought that one is separate from God. It would be possible for anyone who had that thought to write something deceptive. In other words, you cannot be separate from God. *If* there is a belief that you are separate at the center of a thought system, the whole thing can be deceptive.

Maybe it is time to re-examine all of our religious conditioning, keeping that which feels appropriate, and forgiving that which was confusing and mixed with the ego. The *Course* is not a religion or path. It is a correction.

Ken Wapnick is one of the world's leading experts on *A Course in Miracles*, and a respected teacher of mine. He has shared that the presence of Jesus on the planet was so pure and purged so much ego that it has taken 2,000 years to process it. Now, after all this time, we are ready to hear the next words from Him. Now, He is saying,

"You didn't understand before; I am going to give you another chance. I will explain it again; and so, here is a course in miracles. *A Course in Miracles* IS a miracle. The answers you have wanting are in there. The solutions to your problems are in there. The way to heal yourself totally is in there. The way to have a perfect holy relationship is in there. The way to have world peace is in there. What more do we want? Nothing. Now we have the answers. All we have to do is have the willingness to read it.

Why would someone not read it? Maybe they are on a different path and that is fine. It is not for everyone. Maybe you are one of those who have never heard of it. Well, if so, I am honored to have the opportunity to tell you about it. But what if it is for you and you are just resisting it? Then ask yourself these questions:

• Am I just afraid of having it all and feeling good?

• Am I choosing pain over joy?

• Am I too addicted to my negativity to recognize a good thing like this?

• Am I angry at God and fed up with anything in a religious tone?

• Am I being stubborn and rebellious and loving my misery?

If you answer yes to any of these questions, you may have convinced yourself you do not need the *Course* and/or you should not read it. All I am asking is if you are willing to see this differently?

The way I found the *Course* was a friend sent me xeroxed copies of the first few chapters. I will always be grateful for this. I bought the books immediately. I might have delayed otherwise.

If you have never bought the books, I hope you will open them now. If you have bought them and have never opened them, I hope you will now. (I do recommend that people sleep with the books if they can't seem to open them. The vibration of the words will eventually penetrate enough so that one day you will roll over and open them.)

There may be a tremendous resistance to the *Course* at first. This is just your ego. Go beyond it. As your ego dissolves you will begin to see how the books make a lot of sense. Then later you will probably say, "This is the *only* thing that makes any sense." From time to time you may avoid them, but you will never forget them. And eventually you will crave them in a happy, wonderful way.

The *Course* should be read according to the directions in the *Teacher's Manual.* It is designed perfectly, and this should be honored. Reading ahead to parts for which one has not had proper preparation may stir up too much ego and cause discomfort. To make it easier on yourself, you might find it helpful to join a local study group. In order to grasp the context of the *Text,* I have written the book *Drinking the Divine* which you may find helpful. It is a study guide, and not meant to replace the *Course.* It was written to clarify the main points of each chapter and to facilitate the *Text.*

To give you an idea of what the text is like, I am going to randomly choose one paragraph from the pages that I read today. Every paragraph is equally powerful. Notice how much "food for thought" is here. Be willing to digest it for awhile. This paragraph is loaded, as is every paragraph.

> *No right mind can believe that its will is stronger than God's. If, then, a mind believes that its will is different from Him, it can only decide either that there is no God or that God's will is fearful. The former accounts for the atheist and the latter for the martyr, who believes that God demands sacrifices. Either of these insane decisions will induce panic, because the atheist believes that he is alone, and the martyr that God is crucifying him.*

Now let us take an example of a workbook lesson. (There are 365 lessons, one for each day of the year.) One of the things that helped me to remember to do a lesson each day was to write the line in the palm of my hand in ballpoint pen. Then, I would at least notice it from time to time. Often people would ask me what that was, and that would give me an opportunity to share about the *Course.* Today I chose lesson #190 just as an example. I chose this one because it applies to the name of this book. The lesson is this:

I CHOOSE THE JOY OF GOD INSTEAD OF PAIN . . .

What does this mean? It means, first of all, that we can and do choose either joy or pain. It is up to us. The lesson goes on to explain that it is our thoughts alone that cause us pain. The explanation is beautiful:

> *Pain means one is mistaken in his thinking. If one is in pain, it is a sign that in his mind illusions are reigning. He is indulging in the ego. The main point is that nothing external can hurt you. Only your mind. No one but yourself affects you. There is nothing in the world that has the power to dominate you, make you ill or sad. But it is you who has the power to dominate all things. The world you see does nothing. It merely represents your thoughts and it will change as your change your mind . . . and choose the joy of God as what you want. When one is in pain, one is denying God. But if you do lay down your thoughts of danger and fear and attack and judgment of yourself, you will begin to find a world without pain. You will begin to find the joy of God. Pain is illusion. Joy is reality. Pain is deception, joy alone is truth. And so again we make the only choice that ever can be made; we choose between illusions and the truth, or pain and joy, or Hell and Heaven. Let our gratitude unto our Teacher fill our hearts, as we are free to choose our joy instead of pain, our holiness in place of sin, the peace of God instead of conflict, and the light of Heaven for the darkness of the world (excerpt from* A Course in Miracles, *Lesson 190, page 352).*

I want to acknowledge you for reading this chapter. I want to acknowledge you for your openness to the *Course.* And I pray that you are one of those who actually will pursue it for the rest of your life, and I thank you in advance if that is you.

Fasting

People usually think that fasting is hard and boring. I'd like to offer you another approach—it can actually be fun and easy. First, you must let go of all your negative thoughts and belief systems about fasting. Be willing to see this differently. Imagine that this is the first time you have heard of it. As with anything, your experience of fasting will depend upon what your thoughts about it are. If you think it will be difficult, it probably will. Then you would do well to give up all thoughts such as, "I need three meals a day in order to survive."

If you read my book, *The Only Diet There Is,* you will see there are people who eat almost nothing at all. They live on the light of God. (It *is* good to be clear on the lesson from *A Course in Miracles,* "I am sustained by the love of God.") Fasting is frequently recommended in the Bible. It is a good way of loving God because you are purifying your body and can therefore channel much more of God's love and energy. You can do better at everything.

In my experience, when I have really committed to fasting, I have always received tremendous spiritual rewards and surprises. This is not a reason for doing it, but rather, a by-product of the purity obtained.

You can begin by fasting on juice one day a week. Then increase it to two days, on occasion. For me it is easier to do a five day fast than one or two days, because I know that I am really going to *go for it;* and that way I back up my thoughts and I get more out of it. To me, the real value comes after the third day. This is when you begin to get the supreme benefits. And if you can go on to 10 days, you can be fairly sure that something will transform in you after the sixth day.

Most people are tempted to quit after the seocnd day. This is a shame, because it is really only the first two days that are hard. About the third day, in my experience, you tend to forget about food and begin to experience the lack of desire to eat. This is when it becomes fun and interesting. Do not deny yourself the pleasure of this experience. Of course, I do admit that this is all easier if you are in a special setting. If you are doing your usual work routine, fasting may require more fortitude, especially if your friends keep inviting you out to eat and you go. Even this, however, can be done. I deliberately tried that once. I accepted all restaurant invitations and had consumme or nothing. It did give me a sense of satisfaction, but it may be preferable to do it another way.

If you would like to read about different fasts, then I recommend the book, *"Are You Confused?"* You could start on the Master Cleanser fast, which is a drink made of pure water, lemon juice, maple syrup, and cayenne. You can carry this with you all day in a bottle and sip it. I experienced no hunger at all.

Another fast I like is to simply drink fresh fruit juices. While writing this book, I went on a vegetable juice fast which I found very rewarding. I put carrots, celery, parsley, and spinach leaves together in the juicer. It is a very refreshing and nourishing drink.

The longest I fasted on liquids alone (broth and juice) was for 30 days. I was amazed that I never got hungry, tired, or weak. What I did get, however, was angry. I am sure that is why my guru suggested I do this assignment; it brought up and out my suppressed anger.

I deliberately do not fast to lose weight, although you can do that, and it works. I try to fast only for spiritual reasons and then it seems like a reward instead of a punishment. I am convinced that that is why fasting is fun and easy for me and why I like it so much. If I felt that I had to fast as a deprivation or punishment, or I put pressure on myself, then I know it would not be the same kind of experience at all. I cannot stress enough the importance of the motive, the attitude, the way of thinking with which you approach fasting.

If you tune into your body, it will tell you when you need to fast. Fasting, for example, every Monday would be good. However, I am now referring to longer fasts which should be done periodically— every three months, for example, or whenever your body tells you to. Or when you are not feeling right, or when things are not going well.

If you are a leader or head of a company, you will be amazed how this kind of thing will affect your whole business. When I go away into solitude and fast, my whole staff cleans up. I don't even have to say anything. They automatically begin to clean desks, clean up the filing, shape everything up. Their communication gets cleaner and everyone is happier. This is the psychic effect, and it is wonderful.

If one person in a family begins to clean up, the rest are automatically affected. You become an inspiration to them; your love of yourself and God begins to radiate. You begin to move a lot of energy and you begin to see the results all around you.

Solitude

Solitude is one of the best ways I know to be spiritually nourished. It is very different from being lonely, although many people are afraid to choose solitude because they are afraid of being lonely. And yet, you must learn to live with yourself before you can expect anyone to really live with you. So solitude can be an *end* to loneliness. When you master solitude, many people will want to be with you.

In solitude you can clear the thoughts that make your life difficult. People may be afraid of solitude because they are afraid of their own thoughts! But once you are enlightened and you know you can easily change your negative thoughts to positive ones, there is nothing to be afraid of. You can be in charge of your mind and your feelings. You will have an opportunity, like never before, to observe your mind. In solitude, you are not distracted as much from your own divinity. There is an exquisite opportunity to remember your connection to God. You begin to talk with God naturally whereas other times you may have forgotten. You may finally begin to listen to the voice of the Holy Spirit in solitude, that voice that knows your higher good, that voice that guides you perfectly. That Voice that leads you back to joy. Often in solitude, your dreams become more vivid, more exciting, more liberating, and more instructive. You become more psychic. New ideas come to you. New ways of clearing problems. You become more and more creative. Your body starts clearing itself. Your feelings become more sensitive. Everything is more real and exquisite. You get to know yourself better and trust yourself more, and this raises your self-esteem. In solitude, one is often inspired to fast, meditate, or do other disciplines. These, with the proper attitude, are guaranteed to bring joy.

In the beginning, you can start out with one day a week for solitude. Do not see anyone, do not listen to TV, radio, or anything. It is better not even to read books at first, or to write. It is best to do nothing. It is my opinion that your first experiences in solitude should be away from your own home. A beautiful spot would be ideal. Someone's cabin or guest house would be good, or even consider checking into a nice hotel room. It is important to be away from constant distractions. Gradually increase the number of days. It would be good to try four straight days of solitude as the next "stretch" for yourself.

Eventually, you want to give yourself the experience of one full week in solitude. You will be simply amazed by what happens when you can commit yourself for that long. Then you begin to open yourself up to more mystical experiences, religious experiences, if you will, holy encounters perhaps on the astral plane; all those things you have heard about that you wonder why may not have happened to you. The stage must be set. Communion with God is essential.

The longest period I have been able to achieve is six weeks. During this time, I went away to Bali. Occasionally, I spoke to Balinese people to get around, etc.; however, I was, for the most part, completely in solitude, working on the book, *Drinking the Divine*. Yes, there were times I went through a lot, but mostly I was in bliss, because I was not distracted from reading *A Course in Miracles*. Solitude is the right time to study spiritual literature. It goes in deeper. It penetrates you, puts you in bliss.

Well, all I can say is, "don't knock it until you try it."

Prayer

The best time to do spiritual practices is between 4:30 a.m. and 7:00 a.m. This will give quick, maximum spiritual progress. Immediately after getting up, take a bath or shower.

It often helps to keep a picture of your favorite Deity or teacher in front of you. Side by side with *japa* (repeating God's name), think of the Lord as present before you and picture His beauty.

Entertain the attitude of a servant while doing *japa*. Have a separate meditation room with an altar. If this is not possible, then at least a corner of a room set apart with a screen or curtain.

After *japa* is over, do not immediately leave the place; do not mix with everyone or plunge right into worldly activity. Take some time to integrate and experience your feelings and sensations.

A lot of people have given up on prayer, thinking that they have not received what they asked for. I hope that I can inspire you to look at the matter of prayer once again. First of all, if you have asked for something and not received it, maybe you need to know why. Either you were blocking on the receiving end (with some unconscious negative thought you were not aware of); or you had too much fear of receiving what you asked for; or, what you asked for wasn't really good for you and your higher self knew it.

Let's say you ask for something but you have too much fear of receiving it. What you need to know is that the Holy Spirit will *not* add to your fear, and therefore it would not be good for you to have this until your fear is worked out. *A Course in Miracles* explains it this way: Let's say you are praying for an overnight healing of a certain disease. However, a sudden miracle may be such a threat to your thought system that you cannot allow this to happen for yourself. What you need to pray for first is release of the fear of having a miracle. Ultimately, pray for help in the resolution of the cause of your fear (which is the belief in separation).

So, when your prayers are not answered, do not blame God. *Only you can deprive yourself of anything.* The source is abundant and wants to give to you. The giver expands by giving. God wants you to have all the gifts of the Kingdom.

The initial phase of prayer is one of emptying. Pouring out the contents of the heart ("emptying the cup")—without editing or embarrassment, withholding nothing—is a pre-requisite to attain perfection in prayer. In the privacy of one's inner sanctum, a complete housecleaning of all afflicting emotions must be achieved before there is room for God's grace.

One of the methods of prayer that I learned as a child is very effective. It contains five parts:

1. Opening
2. Forgiveness
3. Gratitude
4. Petition
5. Closing

1. *Opening:* This is for setting the stage, creating the ambiance, establishing the connection: Read from the scriptures or from spiritual and/or metaphysical books . . . for example, this would be a good time to read three pages from *A Course in Miracles, Text.*

2. *Forgiveness:* This is where you ask for pardon for anything you feel is your wrongdoing. You also ask to be forgiven by any specific person, or you forgive someone you need to forgive.

3. *Gratitude:* This is where you specifically express gratitude for the things you have, for friends, for love, for the life you have, for your health, etc. Remember that what you have gratitude for increases.

4. *Petition:* Now you are in the proper context to ask for help or guidance in any specific area . . . Talk to the Holy Spirit freely, knowing, having faith that you will receive help.

5. *Closing:* This, again, is when you read spiritual literature as above. My suggestion at this point would be to read your *Course in Miracles* lesson for the day.

This prayer technique can be done alone or in groups.

It is very good to do it aloud with friends. This is especially effective as a daily ritual in families. I have given this prayer ritual to couples who were in stress in their marriage and on the verge of divorce; and they have reported to me that it saved their marriage. I have mentioned this technique in my other books, but it is worth repeating.

Of course, asking and begging is a low form of prayer. The highest form of prayer is gratitude for and celebration of your connection to the Source. I refer you to *A Course in Miracles* sequel called "Song of Prayer." I will quote a few paragraphs here.

> *Prayer is practice of the presence of God. A thankful mind attracts good. Try to get to the point where you are then giving thanks instead of complaining/fearing/or worrying.*
>
> *If you do petition, pray from the standpoint of already having what you ask for. (KNOWING THAT THERE IS NO SPIRITUAL LACK.) Give thanks, then, that it is already done!*
> 1. *Lay hold of the good you desire.*
> 2. *Recognize it is here and now.*
> 3. *Have absolute confidence.*
> 4. *Express gratitude.*

Ask, and BELIEVING, you shall receive. Faith is everything. When you develop a consciousness of the things you seek, they will appear in your presence. God meets you on the level of your consciousness. If your consciousness of need is greater than your consciousness of God, then need will expand. That is because what you think about expands. WHEN YOU LOVE GOD MORE THAN YOUR PROBLEM, YOU WILL BE HEALED. YOUR PRAYERS WILL BE ANSWERED. God can work through you only when your consciousness and His are One . . . when you stop forgetting that Creator and Created are One . . . when you are conscious of your oneness with God, then you embody Him. Prayer does help clear the way for acceptance of your Oneness, yes; and yet, the more you accept the Oneness before prayer, the better will be your response from prayer.

Affirmations are also like prayers that you impress onto Infinite Spirit to create a desired result. Always thinking in affirmations will keep you in a constant state of prayer.

I find it very effective to talk out loud to God when I am praying. Again, this can feel embarrassing at first, just as kneeling might. However, try it. It helps you to stay conscious, produces more feeling and reality to your relationship with God, and I have found it to be a very deep experience. Do this in the woods by yourself or even right in your bedroom while lying down and before or after your meditation. For my prayers, I usually write and mail my guru Babaji letters, and talk to Jesus out loud. I don't know why this is, but it always works for me. They all answer me in their different ways. God speaks through everyone.

Ho O Pono Pono

It is my great honor and privilege to be able to introduce you to the ancient Hawaiian technique called Ho O Pono Pono. I truly thank Morrnah Simeona, supreme Kahuna, for giving me permission to share this with you now.

This technique, a combination of special Hawaiian prayers and breathing processes, is one of the sweetest, most gentle and beautiful ways I know of to free and purify oneself. It is a surefire way to clear karma from past lives and release emotional and physical attachments to people, places and things. That is the purpose of the process: Freedom from Bondage.

It can be used to clear your thoughts and therefore heal your body. If you read books on the Huna Religion of the Kahunas, you will find that they knew exactly what they were doing. They could actually heal people instantly, change weather, set bones, affect the elements, and, on occasion, resurrect the dead. I would definitely recommend taking a Ho O Pono Pono class and learning this technique for yourself. (Information on when and where classes will be held in your area can be obtained by writing: "Foundation of the I," Attention: Connie Weber, U.S. Coordinator, 261 Stanton Avenue, Plymouth Meeting, PA. Phone: (215) 825-2075.)

Rebirthing

I love talking about Rebirthing. Rebirthing healed me. It is a spiritual gift. It is one of the main purification tools we use in the LRT Ohana to produce Joy. What it does is help you release the blocks you have that keep you from experiencing your natural state, which *IS* Joy. This happens through the power of using your own breath . . . it is connecting the inhale with the exhale in a relaxed, intuitive rhythm. Rebirthing is not a discipline, it is an inspiration. It cleanses your mind and body in a very dynamic way with Divine Energy.

Rebirthing acquaints you with a dimension of spiritual energy which you may never have experienced. It can be an ultimate healing experience because breath, together with quality of thoughts, can produce miracles.

In the beginning we used it to remember and re-experience our birth in order to release any trauma that remained. That alone was, and is, simply a remarkable aspect of Rebirthing; but then we found out that it does so much more than just that! Rebirthing can literally transform your subconscious. It creates a safe environment in your mind and body for symptoms of the past to act themselves out . . . in this way you can become free of all negativity.

Rebirthing increases your ability to receive love. It definitely improves your relationships, especially if both you and your partner are getting rebirthed. This adds tremendous joy to your relationship.

Rebirthing can help you to become more creative and intuitive. This happens as you clear your ego, so you can experience the availability of infinite intelligence.

Rebirthing is truly a "rejuvenation process." Your body is rejuvenated with divine energy. This feeling of "being automatically renewed" produces tremendous joy in the rebirthee and is very rewarding to the rebirther as well.

Rebirthing is sacred. To me, it is a way in which you can experience "making love to God"—because you are communing with the Holy Spirit.

When I was healed through the Rebirthing process, I was so ecstatic about the results that I gave up everything that I had been doing and I gladly began traveling all around the world to tell everyone of the benefits. Others who try it feel the same. Many people tell us that Rebirthing is the greatest experience they have had since they were born! We constantly hear comments like this:

"Every growth experience I have had promised more than it delivered except Rebirthing. Rebirthing delivered a whole lot *more* than it promised."

The Rebirthing process is explained in depth in my books *Celebration of Breath* and *Rebirthing in the New Age*. It is also summarized in the back of my book *Loving Relationships*. To me, it is one of the most important things to commit to, to experience Pure Joy.

A minimum of 10 sessions with the same well-trained rebirther is recommended (eventually you can learn to rebirth yourself). Rebirthing, for us, is considered a lifelong process that helps us stay pure. Once you get past the original 10 sessions, things get so interesting, and you experience so much change, that you really want to go on and on and on . . .

Top Rebirthers are available at every Loving Relationships Training (LRT) Center. For information, call our toll free number: 1-800-INTL-LRT.

Indian Sweat Lodge

One of the great traditions of the American Indians is the Sweat Lodge. This is an unforgettable experience, especially when done with people that you know in a group seminar or outing.

Usually, this ritual occurs in an appropriate, beautiful, outdoor wooded setting, preferably by a cold river stream. The sweat itself is done in a low igloo-like tent holding about 30 people, usually sitting in two circles around the fire pit. The large rocks for the fire are prepared early in the morning by the team who runs the sweats. These rocks "cook" underground in a fire and therefore they come out literally red hot.

Before you go in, you are usually encouraged to fast. When you gather around the fire to share, there may be a ceremony led by the medicine man or medicine woman, wherein you pass around a peace pipe and recite prayers. Sometimes there is a ceremony whereby you place your most sacred objects on a mound to be blessed by a medicine man. They are left on the mound during the sweat.

When it is time to enter the sweat lodge, usually a medicine man or his most direct assistant will say prayers over you and clear your aura with Eagle feathers as you crawl in. The medicine man goes in first and clears the space; you follow him and sit quietly until everyone is settled. Then he begins prayers and/or chants . . . to evoke the Great Spirit. The hot rocks are brought in on a pitchfork. When the pit is filled with the rocks, the flap is put down and no one can enter. (It is dark except for the glow from the rocks.)

Then the medicine man usually grates some sacred root and throws it on the fire. Sparks fly, and the aroma envelopes you as the medicine man reminds you that you are all one. He begins to throw water on the rocks while chanting. Then you sweat. He chants, you sweat. You sweat, he chants. This continues for about 20 minutes. Some people cry as they let go. Everyone breathes a lot and sometimes someone will get the urge to run out. (Usually his surrounding peers support him through that; but you could leave if you absolutely needed to.) Finally, the medicine man throws open the flap, and everyone runs to the cold river stream and immerses. This is exquisite. This cycle is then repeated two more times.

I did my first sweat with the LRT staff and it was mixed—men and women. In Europe, I did a sweat with only women, and the men went with only men. This was very sweet and unique, and of course, intimate in a wonderful way. The feeling was totally different. I recommend you try both. In my second sweat, we did not come out for breaks in a river. I was not sure people could do it, but many went all three rounds, and it was amazing.

The feeling of purity after a sweat is something to behold. In the LRT Spiritual Retreats, I try to take advantage of this wonderful feeling and level of intimacy by having the group come together and share their experiences.

I feel that it is very important that a sweat be done properly, with the appropriate guides, spiritual aspects, and rituals. Therefore, I would definitely recommend that a true Indian Medicine Man be present to lead the experience.

Fire Purification

Fire purification is an ancient technique for clearing one's aura and one's karma, and for releasing anger, guilt, and so on. It is quite simple—all you have to do is meditate on the fire with your eyes open. This can be done with a fireplace, an open bonfire, or, lacking these, even with a candle. Meditate on the fire at the level of the navel to gain immense strength.

Babaji taught us to meditate on the elements. He also taught us the ancient "fire ceremony," where you feed the fire with fruits, foods, incense, and flowers to return your gratitude to the Source. Prayers and mantras are recited by the High Priest during this ceremony, which, if done properly, is also a ceremony for world peace. This is always done at Babaji's ashram in India, and we try to do it at the Spiritual Retreats—if we can get appropriate fire permits. Often we do an all night meditation outside around the fire in silence. This is very powerful. Sleep deprivation is another method of purification, by the way. Try standing up all night once a month and meditating on a fire!

About this technique, Babaji says:

> *Worshipping the Fire means worshipping the inner light. Worshipping the Fire burns Karma. It is spiritual purification. Worshipping the Fire transforms into Pure Love all that is impure in the heart and mind. The power of the Holy Fire, the flame of Love unfolds the qualities of the Soul.*

Bodywork

Since the mind rules the body, the body can be cleared by using the mind. Sometimes body work can assist in speeding up this process. Anything that makes you feel good, loved, innocent, and whole is right, and, therefore, body work can be a way of loving God. The better you feel, the more you can express your divinity.

I would recommend the following types of body work to help you feel better:

* Massage
* Rolfing
* Body Harmony
* Chiropractic
* Shiatsu
* Treger work

Use discrimination in picking a body worker. If you spend time purifying yourself with Rebirthing, chanting, the *Course*, and so on, and then you use a body worker who is very negative and rough, you are defeating your purpose. Find a body worker who also loves God, who seems holy and graceful—one who is enlightened himself and choosing life and joy, one who is breathing a lot. You want one who *increases* your positive vibrations.

We have recommended body workers in each of the LRT Ohana centers. You can call a center and find out who my personal body workers are in that city.

I would like to acknowledge my regular, personal body workers who have helped to keep me in such good health and joy. Although

I have some in each city, these have been the ones I have seen the most often:

- Don McFarland for body harmony
- Patrick Collard for body thought release
- Kermit Stick for rolfing
- Dr. Michael Faila and Dr. Joseph Adler for chiropractic
- Terry Milligan for past life work and adjustments

The Work of Patrick Collard

When I took my friend Patrick Collard to see a clairvoyant in Stockholm, the clairvoyant said she had never seen so much light pouring out of anyone's hands in her life as she saw coming from Patrick's hands! I understood this because I had experienced it when he did body work on me. I had also experienced over and over again lines of people, myself included, waiting hours and hours to be seen by Patrick. This light for healing is not the only gift that Patrick has. Because of the very unusual circumstances of his birth (he was born with the cord around his neck) his brain apparently overcompensated for the fact that he had extreme stifling of left brain activity, resulting in stronger right brain activity. He realized this gift of "seeing and sensing" with his right brain at a very early age. By clearing his mind and focusing on the right brain, he is able to become very receptive to a person's thoughts and feelings and how they manifest in the body. He is then able to receive a complete view of the body and recognize what that person's mind wishes to release from the body at that time.

The entire basis of his work focuses on the fact that absolutely *all* disorders, disease and illness of the body are a result of the mind's disorder. An ill or diseased thought creates an ill or diseased body. His skill is to find the thought, release the thought, and support the body in carrying out its natural function. The body, being a self-healing, perfectly-tuned system, carries out the commands of the mind. Patrick, being very clairvoyant, can "see" the thoughts and "see" where they are in the body. Patrick helps provide the means for the

Higher Self to communicate to the body and mind in order to restore harmony on mental, emotional, physical and spiritual levels. He awakens people to the reality of unity or "no separation" between these levels. Balance of vision creates healthy communication which creates healthy results.

Patrick himself has been a real gift to me and the LRT staff, and I would like to publicly acknowledge him for this contribution to us. He is usually traveling with me, or around the LRT centers, and can be reached through the LRT International Office. He also teaches seminars on how to develop this ability in oneself. The toll-free number of the International LRT office is 1-800-INTL-LRT. When he is not traveling, Patrick's home contact is: Patrick Collard, 413 Avenida Teresa, San Clemente, CA 92672.

I would like to acknowledge all the healers and body workers who have contributed to my well-being over the years. It has all helped me tremendously to maintain my excellent health while dealing with a very intense schedule of constant travel. I have been able to handle this remarkably well, partly because of this support.

If this acknowledgment reaches any of you whom I have met in my travels, I would like to honor you by saying *Thank You!*

I welcome more people in the healing arts who would like to serve the OHANA (LRT communities of the world). There is an abundance of work to be done in helping people to experience Pure Joy in their bodies.

Body Harmony

I strongly recommend this type of body therapy for many reasons. It is wonderful for you. It is very modern and very "new age," and it is probably what you have been looking for to get your body "handled" painlessly. It can help you to release traumas, relax stress, relieve pain and restore natural body posture and function. It is very subtle and profound.

Our historical traumas are publicly displayed in our bodies, and these unresolved situations compress our tissues. These incompletions impinge on the possibilities of today . . . But, there IS a way out! There are processes to unwind our historical limitations. Body Harmony is one of those. Body Harmony is a pleasurable experience that leaves you with a permanent change.

One of the reasons I like it so much is because it is in harmony with Rebirthing, which is the main tool we use for spiritual purification in our community. Rebirthing changes your body and mind through working on the inside, while Body Harmony also changes your body and mind, but through working on the outside. Through working from two directions, you get quicker results.

Another reason I like it is because it was created by Don McFarland, a wonderful friend of mine who has given me years of fantastic body work. I feel I am a "result" of body harmony (along with everything else in this book), and I thank Don and all the other body workers mentioned in this chapter.

Don evolved this work from a multitude of practices and insights of healers and shamans from all corners of the globe. It seems to combine the best of everything. The result: freedom, liberations, feeling good, expansion, harmony! (According to Don, it is also a spiritual process to remind our tissues of the glory of *NOW*.)

One night I had a dream that I was running down the street escaping from my past. I accidentally ran up an alley that was a dead end. At the end of the alley there was a band playing a tune just for me. The tune was called "Harmony," and it was in celebration of the fact that my body was finally in harmony. I felt incredibly happy and alive. I called Don the next morning to report this. He was astounded, as he had just decided that he should call his work body harmony. (I had not known this.) For him, the dream was a clear verification.

On a recent trip to Peru, Don and I were meditating together in a cave deep inside the Inca ruins of Macchu Picchu. He was receiving all kinds of new insights and understandings about the body and his work. It was exciting to watch as his body was spontaneously "moved" by some powerful force. I received the message that people should learn to give body harmony to each other; just like they should learn to Rebirth each other. The message was, "This will be super important for people in the unstable decades ahead." So that is why I am taking the time to write this report on body harmony. It is time that we all begin to operate at maximum efficiency. For information call (213) 393-6900.

Shaving Your Head (Headshave)

Another thing that will purify you rapidly is Headshave. Notice your reaction and all that comes up for you just hearing that word! Now, imagine all that would come up for you if you actually did it, which is exactly the point. If you want an extreme, rapid, surefire purification, this could be it. Again, this may not be for everyone.

For me, it was one of the most religious experiences of my life, and it opened me up greatly. (It is also a certain kind of "initiation" if you are a devotee of Babaji.) This ritual has been done for thousands of years and so, obviously, it must be of value. Shaving your head (and this includes to the skin with a razor blade) is a very personal, deep experience between you and God. It is something you choose. Babaji certainly never *made* me do it.

In the LRT Spiritual Retreat, we offer the opportunity to shave your head—optional, of course; and usually one or two people choose to do it. We then create a beautiful ceremony where the whole group chants, and I usually begin the shave, and then people who are close to that person will continue it.

For me, it was a symbolic act whereby I was saying to God, "Look, I am going to try to surrender as much as possible to you and in this act, I am demonstrating that *willingness.*"

I have written about my headshaving experiences in other books. I remain very happy that I did it, and I would definitely consider doing it once a decade. At Babaji's ashram, the tradition is to leave it shaved for nine entire months (the period of the womb) for one to get the full benefit. I am also very happy that I followed that rule. I can sincerely say that it was a very personal act of loving God, and resulted in tremendous joy. Not only did it open me up and purify me, but also, because I learned so much about myself, it increased my self love and commitment.

It can be done in a barber shop, yes, but I would say: do not deprive yourself of the glory of having this be a deep spiritual ritual. It is best, in my opinion, when done in that context.

Mundan (headshave) is a radical method of altering one's false identification with a body. We are so used to seeing ourselves appear one way as we look in a mirror . . . Mundan changes that immediately. It gives us the chance to see that "something" in us that appears constant, regardless of any change in the physical. Mundan stimulates all the psychic centers on the head and creates a singular unit of cosmic reception (devoid of thousands of hairs) that has a clearer relationship with universal vibratory state.—Ram Dass Giri.

Visiting Holy Places and India

One thing I would say to all seekers who want to enjoy loving God more is, do not overlook the possibility of going to India, at least once in your life. This, I admit, is my very biased opinion, being a great lover of India and what it can do for you, and having been there seven times. To me, India is the Mother, the Divine Mother herself. In my experience, the minute you set foot on her land, something profound begins to change in you . . . and you can never be the same again. The whole country is like an ashram. There, even though on the surface it does not *look* pure, it will purify you in surprising ways. When you see beyond the dirt, you see so much love, humility, devotion to God, and glory that you cannot help but surrender. Usually the first thing that happens is the Western Mind collapses. There is nothing to hang on to. This breaking down of your "form" is just the beginning. And then, *if* you go to an ashram, your life may really be turned around.

It was in the ashram that I truly learned to love God. Never have I encountered such an intense stripping of the ego. When I saw what the saints were really like, I was forever challenged to even begin matching their devotion . . . it is something I always long for. For me, to be in the presence of my guru Babaji was the most intensely joyous, all-encompassing, all pervading, marvelous experience of my life. I have written about my relationships with Babaji in India in the forthcoming book *INTERLUDES WITH THE GODS*. There is information about Him in Part V of this book. If you are at all interested in visiting Babaji's ashram in India, you may write for instructions to the following address:

The Ashram of Sri Shri 1008 Bhagwan Herakhan
Wale Baba P.O. Herakhan Vishva Mahadham
Via Kathgodam District
Nanital U.P.
Pine Code 263126

Or contact the International LRT office to see if there is a possibility of my taking a group with me, which occurs every year in the Fall (1-800-INTL LRT).

In or out of India, I always recommend visiting ancient temples and religious sites. Especially if there has been centuries of chanting and praying going on in the area. You will benefit from the vibrations. Don't be surprised, however, if you go through a lot of changes before you even get there. You may think you just saw a bunch of buildings. It is so much more—it is the energy of loving God within this place that will purify you. It is that energy that will inspire you to love God more and add to your joy.

WHY GO TO INDIA?

India was the motherland of our race, and Sanskrit the mother of Europe's languages: she was the mother of our philosophy; mother, through the Arabs, of much of our mathematics; mother, through the Buddha, of the ideals embodied in Christianity; mother, through the village community, of self-government and democracy. Mother India is in many ways the mother of us all . . ."

—Will Durant

Other Spiritual Purification Techniques

There are many many ways of purifying oneself that I haven't discussed. Some you might consider are:
• Silence
• Sleep Reduction
• Colonics
• Float to Relax Tanks
• Yoga, Tai Chi, etc.
• The Forgiveness Diet (See *The Only Diet There Is*)
• Celibacy
• Karma Yoga (Work as a form of worship/Work to clear your karma)
• Travel (Especially international travel which helps clear Past Lives)
• Writing (Example: Sentence completion process
"The reasons I feel bad right now are . . ."
"The negative thoughts that cause this pain are . . . "
"What I am really feeling right now is . . . "

Undoubtedly you could add more purification techniques to this chapter. I have covered those that I have tried effectively and encourage you to make up your own methods of purification.

I have integrated these techniques into my life so that they have become "a way of life." They are effortless, natural, fun and easy for me to remember to do. I have trained my mind to gravitate toward the methods I have discussed whenever I feel stuck, tired or confused. I like having a variety to choose from, and often use them in combination.

Spiritual solutions are very pleasurable indeed.

CHAPTER 3
THE OHANA AS A LIFE-LONG SPIRITUAL FAMILY

OHANA is a Hawaiian word that means "extended family." It also means "a chosen family which breathes together ("ha" means breath). It seemed like the perfect word to use to describe what I wanted to have in the Loving Relationships Training Community. I wanted to have a group of people who felt they belonged to a spiritual family as opposed to an organization. I wanted people to feel that they were being empowered by each other to become all they could be: the "multiple guru" system. We are all teachers and all students. I wanted people to feel the joy of belonging to a "healed family," a "chosen family." This we have manifested successfully and are continuing to expand upon—and improve. It is a family dedicated to life itself.

There is a great joy in having the help of others who care about your personal enlightenment and joy as much as you do. It is a relief not to have to do it all alone. It is much more rapid to have a spiritual family. It is much more fun. It is nurturing. It is enlivening. It is more creative. It is more releasing and liberating. We have always maintained the policy of "telling the complete truth faster" . . . and "no withholds" (withheld communications). Everything is out in the open. Everyone helps everyone else with their personal problems in their relationships, bodies, and careers. Everyone is good about sharing new knowledge with each other.

We have 14 LRT centers around the world where you can go and become an immediate part of the Ohana. If you visit any of the following cities, you can call the center manager and tell them you have read my books and want to be a part of the Ohana. We welcome you to participate; and with great joy, we look forward to meeting you.

In the United States:
- New York, New York
- Philadephia, Pennsylvania
- Atlanta, Georgia
- Denver, Colorado
- Los Angeles, California
- Seattle, Washington
- Anchorage, Alaska
    In Europe:
- London, England
- Stockholm, Sweden
- Tel Aviv, Israel
- Madrid, Spain
    In Australia:
- Auckland, New Zealand
- Melbourne
- Sydney

To find the name and number in these locations, please call our toll free number 1-800-INTL-LRT.

The Difference Between a Cult And a True Spiritual Family

Many people are frightened by the idea of a spiritual family because of their fear of cults. There are major differences between a true spiritual family and a cult.

In a cult there is one leader who is supposedly "all powerful"—who makes all decisions to which the group must comply. There is a feeling of dictatorship.

In a true spiritual family, there is group leadership. There is no special guru. Anyone who has the highest thought can be a leader at any time. More experienced people may form small groups; however, they are always training everyone in the group to become leaders. Everyone is a teacher and a student at the same time. The highest spiritual thought rules. Everyone in the group agrees to give up lower thoughts and surrender to the highest thought. There is no "investment" in who originates this thought. This prevents control, manipulation, and coercion. Spiritual purification techniques are used by the group (totally by individual choice) to purify the tendency to use lower thoughts or control tactics. Everyone is coming from a desire to serve humanity.

In a cult, there is a feeling that you have to give up your power, that you are dependent on the whims of the leader. In a true spiritual family, everyone helps everyone else to gain his own Divinity and spiritual power.

In a cult there is a rejection of the past. The group may be told not to speak to parents and blood family members or other past groups. There is a feeling of rebellion against the past and/or culture.

In a true spiritual family, there is a sincere attempt to heal all past relationships. Healing your relationship with your parents is not only encouraged; it becomes a goal. One works toward feelings of gratitude for the past, turning it all into a "win."

In a cult, there is little diversity. Diversity is seen as a threat. In a true spiritual family, there is unity with diversity. Individuality is encouraged. Uniqueness is enjoyed.

In a cult there may be defensiveness and rigidity. There may be a rigid "psychic wall" around the group, or a group thought that they are better than everyone else. It might be like an exclusive club and entry into this club is selective. Or it may be easy to enter and hard to get out. In a true spiritual family, there should be flexibility. The group knows that ultimately all brothers and sisters in the world are created equal. Everyone is welcome and there is a natural desire to network with other spiritual groups to share enlightenment and responsibility to humanity. One can go in and out as one pleases.

In a cult, the group may be forced to pool all resources. In a spiritual family, free enterprise is thriving and everyone works to raise the prosperity consciousness of the entire group. The group is encouraged to tithe and to make contributions to any group they feel supports humanity.

In a cult, you are thrown out if you disagree. In a true spiritual family, all feedback is expressed freely. Everyone tries to take that feedback to the highest spiritual thought, utilizing it for healing purposes.

In a cult, the group itself is everything. It is focusing on itself. People outside may be suspect. In a true spiritual family, all of humanity matters. Although the initial purpose of joining the family may be for personal growth, it quickly becomes clear that this is not for the purpose of becoming narcissistically self absorbed. After self-introspection, self-clearing, and self-discovery, members are clearly guided to an awareness of their spiritual obligations to others and the planet. This usually happens naturally after one feels clear and joyful . . . one wants to share that. It is explained and understood by the group that nothing real can be increased except by sharing. The group feels committed to sharing enlightenment and peace for all.

In a cult there is a feeling of "brainwashing" and parents may want their children out of there and "deprogrammed." In a true spiritual family, everyone is encouraged to think for themselves. They are taught that their thoughts produce their results; and that they are responsible for everything that happens to them. Parents are usually impressed wth the changes they see in their chldren, and they may want to explore the spiritual family themselves because of this. Sometimes the parents come first and enroll their own children in the spiritual family. It can go either way.

In a cult, there may be a tendency to hide the truth or to have "secrets." In a true spiritual family, everything is exposed. There are no secrets because there is nothing to hide. There are not even any "secret teachings" reseved for a select few as in days gone by. All information is freely shared and everyone helps everyone else to integrate it and use it wisely.

In a cult one may not feel free to report anything that seems unethical. In a true spiritual family, any member has the right to speak up on the subject of ethics or the lack of them. If someone is behaving unethically, this is brought to the attention of that person himself;

and the members help him process his ego. Everything is considered a "spiritual opportunity" instead of something that has to be punished. In a true spiritual family, there are clear checks and balances and there is public peer review.

In a cult there is likely to be fear and/or anger. It may, however, be quite suppressed. In a spiritual family, there is an atmosphere of safety, relaxation, joy, fun and aliveness.

In a cult one does not feel free to leave. In a true spiritual family everyone knows he is there by choice and can leave anytime by choice. He has self-esteem enough to run his own life. There is no sense of being trapped in a true spiritual family.

In a cult there may not be room for people to have any skills greater than the leader. That might be threatening, and talent may be suppressed as a result. In a spiritual family, everyone is encouraged to be all that they can be. If competition and sibling rivalry come up, it is expressed, cleared, and handled. The group process is one that encourages everyone to experience their equality and to enjoy the talents of others. People support each other in getting ahead. A gratitude for exceptional people and talents is there. A gratitude for all of life prevails.

In some cults there may be no mention of God or of spirituality. In a true spiritual family, this is the main point. But God is not a "parental figure." The end of separation is the goal. Oneness is what matters. In other "religious cults" they think that they alone have the sole support of God and no other group does. This is obviously wrong because God is with everyone.

In a cult you are required to fanatically submit to the will of one leader and to his beliefs. In a spiritual family you are encouraged to share your passion for peace and love with the whole world.

In a cult your fanaticism drives you to proselytize others. In a spiritual family you share what you value without investment.

In looking around for an appropriate spiritual family and community, be sure you choose a family that is not a cult.

CHAPTER 4

SPIRITUAL RETREATS

Purification by Spiritual Retreat

Now there is a way that you can practice all these spiritual purifications in one setting—the LRT Spiritual Retreat. This is a week-long or 10-day gathering in a resort that represents a "westernized ashram for modern times" which Babaji asked me to create for the Western world because there is such a great need. The retreat has been held at Mt. Shasta, California, Florida, Bali, India, Glastonbury, England, Southern France, and in Peru. Eventually, we will create our own temple grounds and center where it can be held regularly.

I will share some of my experiences of the first retreats we did. I was tremendously affected by these trainings as a teacher and deeply transformed along with the students. I have seen miracle healings, weddings, and many amazing surprises.

If there is a beautiful resort in your area that you feel might be ideal for the retreats, please let us know. I prefer hot springs and a cold mountain stream. An ocean site is next best. Water is essential for morning immersion rituals. A carpeted hall is necessary, and, obviously, the holier the vibrations, the better.

THE FIRST GOD TRAINING The first LRT Spiritual Retreat was at Mt. Shasta. This was perfect for many reasons. Peter Caddy (Founder of the Findhorn) was there. The mountain itself is therapeutic, rising out of nowhere in the solitude of Northern California, and

51

it makes a strong statement of pure healing energy. Stories of the presence of St. Germain abound, and his energy can be strongly felt. Stewart Mineral Springs are nearby, known since Indian times for their healing waters. I found the recently restored facilities to be perfect for us. There was an Indian Medicine Man available for Indian Sweats and a cold mountain stream. We were even able to do hot and cold wet rebirthing.

One hundred LRT graduates came for the two week retreat. We prepared a tent for the temple room. The routine was simple and intense:

6 AM	Dip in the cold mountain stream, total immersion
7 AM	Chanting the Aarati in the temple in Sanskrit
8 AM	Breakfast
9 - 10 AM	Karma Yoga, blessing the land, serving the land and making things more beautiful everywhere
10:30 AM - Noon	Course in Miracles Studies
Afternoon	Alternating Dry Rebirthing, Wet Rebirthing and Indian Sweats
5 PM	Chanting "Om Namaha Shivai" in the meadow
6 PM	Dinner
Every Evening	Spiritual studies and lectures

By 8 AM, after the cold water and the chanting, everyone was very high. The purifications we did after that were gravy . . . everyone was very happy.

The Indian Sweats were particularly interesting. Charlie Tom, the medicine man, began cooking the rocks early in the morning. We would go into the low igloo-sized tent and sit in a circle. His assistant would bring in the extremely hot, red rocks, and put them in a pit. The flap would go down and we would sit in the dark. Charlie would start chanting. Then he would grate some special celery root and throw it on the fire. Sparks would fly and the aroma would "unite" us. He would chant more, and then throw water on the rocks. We would begin to sweat. Then he would "turn it up." We would be so hot that we would have to put our heads to the ground to cool off. After twenty minutes of this he would hurl open the flap and we would all run out and jump in the cold water stream where it was nice and deep. Then we would go back in for another round . . . and then another round after that. Some even stayed on for a fourth round. It was absolutely purifying.

During the day, we took our meals outdoors on the porch or on the covered bridge over the roaring stream. There was much happiness and sharing. Everyone was getting incredibly close and having miracle healings. I was extremely pleased with the results the first week. One day we took a caravan up the mountainside and had a picnic followed by an impromptu wedding of two Australians who had met in the LRT in Melbourne. Charlie Tom performed a real Indian-style wedding in the woods. I was the flower girl. Later, we laid in the sun in fields of wildflowers and chanted.

One evening, I asked the staff if they wanted to put on a talent show. The Center Managers sneaked into Fred's (my co-leader, Fredric Lehrman) and my bedrooms and borrowed our clothes to dress up in. They performed mimes of us teaching. It was the funniest thing we had seen in years. We laughed for an hour. I was wondering when they had time to write the lines and memorize them. Later, they told me they had channeled the whole thing. I thought Babaji must have come through them for entertainment. That was the night I decided I would create SHIVA THEATRE. I really got excited about the idea.

One day the whole group spent the entire day in silence and fasting. Many of them had profound major experiences. Late in the evening we gathered at the temple in silence and listened to Tibetan music . . . Tibetan bells recorded in the monastery in Tibet.

We had a second spontaneous wedding—Joe and Yoka. It was the first time I performed a wedding.

The second week, Babaji began showing up in people's dreams and rebirthings. I had received several calls months before the God Training about this . . . people telling me that they had had dreams that Babaji was going to appear at the first God Training. Of course, I was delighted when it began happening.

The very last day I had breakfast with the assistants in the little town of Mt. Shasta. Afterwards, I stopped at the post office with Terry, who was going to pick up a package. It was Saturday, and although the post office was closed, somehow the package department was open. I went in with Terry. There was only one man ahead of us and he looked absolutely "gone." I have never seen anyone dressed so crazy in my life. He had on clothes that no one on earth would ever design. I was *convinced* of that! The pants were yellow and fuschia checked, but the checks did not line up. The shirt was all kinds of stripes that did not line up and looked awful with the pants. The fabric was worse than polyester. He had carrot red hair. He suddenly turned around and faced me. "You know Dennis. He is great, isn't he?" I was shocked this man would know Dennis, a healer we had been working with at the training. "You know Dennis?" I said, surprised. "Yeah," he said, "and I know Yogananda." "Yogananda?" I shrieked. I couldn't believe it. "Yeah, and I know *Babaji.*" "Babaji?" I was really stunned. How could he know these *names* in his condition, let alone have *met* them?

Then he suddenly turned around and said to my friend, "Trouble with your leg, eh?" This surprised me too, as Terry was indeed having a lot of trouble with his leg. "You are a psychic?" I inquired, by now glued to this crazy man. "Yeah, I am a *healer,*" he said, grabbing my arm and showing me his hand. There *was* something extremely unusual about his hands. I could not fathom what it was. Suddenly the lady behind the package department came up . . . where had she been? She returned his package to him, saying it was impossible to send because she could not read the writing. I looked at it, shocked again. The letters were illegible, as if from another planet; they looked like they had been thrown on the package, one by one, and were actually "shaking" and *moving.* It was a bit like a magnet was underneath and shimmering and was clinging to the lines of the letters. That did it. I began to confront him. "How do you expect anyone to *read* this?" I demanded. "Don't worry," he said, punching me lightly. "It is Egyptian." I don't remember what happened after that. Suddenly I was on the other side of the post office glued to this man. I do not remember walking over there with him at all. He was looking right in my eyes saying, "I am making a movie, you know."

"A movie? What is it about?" I had to know. "It is a secret," he replied. Then he got real close to me and stuck his face right up to mine and said, "GAINES, GAINES, GAINES, GAINES." "What is this?" I demanded, "the thought for the day?" "My NAME," he insisted. Then he asked, "When are you coming back? When are you coming back? When are you coming back? When are you coming back?" I had no answer. But why was he repeating everything four times? Suddenly, I was in the car, gasping and saying to Fred, "There is a very strange man in there . . . very strange." And before I knew it, I blurted out, "I think it's Babaji playing tricks on me." "Let's follow him," Fred shouted. We tore around the corner, but he had disappeared into thin air.

I figured it must have been Bababji. He was always playing around with me about fashion and blowing my mind. He could make up a body or borrow someone's. . . and he used to repeat things like that four times. Then I laid on the floor and I knew it was him because this joy came through me that was so profound that I laughed and laughed and laughed and could not stop laughing for 20 mintues.

Later in the afternoon, everyone was packing and getting ready to leave. I was having a Tarot reading on the swinging bridge. Fred came running down the path saying *Gaines* was on the other bridge. I could not believe it! How did he find me? I temporarily forgot it could be Babaji. I approached to find everyone glued to him. He had his nose right up to Dennis's. They were having a heavy debate about UFOs. When I approached, he announced to everyone, "Here comes the Virgo." I certainly had not said anything about that! I wanted to get away. He was reading me straight through and I felt very exposed. When Fred came, he said, "Oh, very broad Channel." Then he introduced his children. They had carrot red hair and looked like they were from outer space. Nobody on the bridge could get that they were even real.

I was trying to duck out. Dennis and I had a healing seminar that night in Eugene, and we were trying to get going. As we got in the car, there was Gaines on the porch eating with these two strange children and an even stranger looking wife. He shouted at me, "Oh, you and Dennis are working in Eugene, eh? I'll be there," he said. And

SONDRA RAY

that was the end of the first God Training. Babaji had come to acknowledge me, blowing my mind again.

AT GLASTONBURY If you have heard little or nothing about Glastonbury, I am happy to expose this mystical place to you. Glastonbury was the birthplace of Christianity in the Western world and even before that, had been a great center of Druidic culture and tradition. People go there because it is said Jesus of Nazareth visited Glastonbury as a young man, and Joseph of Arimathea came there after the crucifixion, bringing the Chalice cup from the Last Supper and vials containing the sweat and blood of Jesus. They go there because of the Arthurian tradition; Camelot Castle is only a few miles away and legend has it that King Arthur was brought there to die after his last battle.

Glastonbury is still significant today. Many believe that the ground itself comes directly from the continent of Atlantis. It is part of the famous Somerset Zodiac, which is ten miles across and thirty miles round, consisting of a circle of effigies depicting the twelve signs of the zodiac. These signs are molded on the earth's surface through the use of hills, streams, roads, canals, and footpaths. In this way, the stars of the constellations above are accurately reduced on the earth below. These signs can only be recognized from heights above 30,000 feet! The construction happened over 4,000 years ago.

Glastonbury lies at the intersection of two of the best known ley lines in Southern England. Ley lines are lines of magnetic force which ancients recognized and used as a means of orienting their temples of worship. It is no coincidence that a great deal of UFO activity is seen at points along the ley line. Every year, thousands of Pilgrims crowd into Glastonbury for religious and mystical celebrations.

The knowledge of the Ancients maintains that there are three major centers of cosmic power on the Earth. These are situated in Tibet, the Holy Land, and Britain.

The center in Tibet, dormant now, was opened first, and represented the Father. The second center, in the Holy Land, represents the son, and has been active for the past two thousand years. The third center, representing the Holy Ghost, is this center which has its heart in Glastonbury. It is said that when a power center is opened, the

Master responsible always visits the next center to be opened. Hence, Jesus of Nazareth came to Glastonbury as a young man, just as the Master who opened Tibet travelled to the Holy Land.

One of the purposes of the Spirit of Glastonbury is to reawaken within Man his former knowledge of the Forces and Beings beyond the frequency of physical life. These are to play an essential part in the evolution of Man in the New Age. Glastonbury is one of those places where one can cross over into other planes of existence more easily than elsewhere while still being in a physical body. Many people have received inspiration at Glastonbury that has transformed their lives. Strong men have been reduced to tears, the supposedly incurable have been cured, the impossible made possible. Once you have subjected yourself to this power you will never be quite the same again.

You can imagine what it might be like to have a spiritual retreat at a power spot like this! Many people experienced deep cleansing and what they called "miracles." One of the miracles we all had was meeting a fellow Immortalist in a most unusual, magical, rather astonishing way. This being, a very gifted Immortal Poet named Robert Coon, touched us all so deeply that we brought him to teach our class for a whole day. This was an unforgettable experience.

CHAPTER 5
MASTERING LIFE

Mastering life will bring you joy. Of course, all my books and the books in the LRT Ohana as well as the LRT itself are for learning how to master life. There are many wonderful books and trainings geared toward this purpose.

There is no longer any reason for being sick, depressed, or miserable. We now have all the techniques available to get you out of misery. The only question is: will you take advantage of them? You must use them in order to get out of misery. It takes a lot of effort, strain, and hard work to create and hang on to misery. Letting it go is always much easier than hanging on to it.

Some people say they don't have the time to do purification techniques, and yet you can get a lot more done in a shorter period of time when you are clear. It used to take me a year to write a book. The time began to shrink to a period of months, and now is a matter of weeks. I have literally saved years by practicing spiritual purification.

As regards cost—the best investment you can make is in yourself. If you take care of yourself, and purify yourself, you can save money through preventing illness. Your work will improve, and you will make more money. Most people tell us that the money they invest in the LRT rapidly comes back to them multiplied. That is because they remove the blocks to receiving love, and when you remove those blocks, you are also removing blocks to receiving money.

Mastering life means that you know with certainty that your thoughts create your results and you are constantly correcting and raising the quality of your thoughts. It means that when you make a mistake you immediately self-correct and continue to love yourself. You find the negative thought you had that created the result and you change it so that you will get a better result next time. Therefore, you keep moving and everything in your life becomes a win. It means that you accept the atonement for yourself. When you are totally and absolutely committed to your own spiritual enlightenment, then you begin to learn how to master life. If you hate life you cannot master it. If you love life, it will begin to work for you.

A Course in Miracles reminds us that in life, "We see what we expect, and we expect what we invite."

Mastering life also means mastering relationships. Perhaps you think that you love God, but not each and every person. Remember this:

> *What you do to a brother (all mankind), you do to God. What you do to a brother, you do to yourself. That is because God has but one son, knowing all as one. No one who condemns a brother can see himself as guiltless and in the peace of God. If your brothers are part of you, will you accept them? When everyone is welcome to you as you would have yourself be welcome to your Father, then and then only will you be without guilt. (CIM, p. 246, Text)*

You cannot enter into a real relationship with *any* of God's sons unless you love them all equally. Love is not special. If you single out a part of the Sonship for your love, you are imposing guilt on all your relationships and making them real. You can love only as God loves. Seek not to love unlike Him for there is no love apart from His. So, this is what the Course has to say: (*CIM*, p. 247, Text). It repeatedly states that you must see only the good and the God in your Brother or else you are making the ego real. The Course goes so far as to say that not only should you love your enemy, your enemy is your savior. He that you have "set up" as your enemy is the one who will show you the part of you that needs healing; and in that way he is saving you from hurting yourself with your own ego.

As we say in the LRT, if there is someone you hate, take them to lunch and find out what *your* problem is, remembering that this person is your teacher, your brother, your potential savior. And for today, practice loving *everyone*.

Part of mastering life is finding the perfect career for yourself, enjoying doing it excellently, and experiencing success at that. One affirmation we give people is this: *I am willing for the Divine Plan of my Life to Manifest.* (This is very powerful as an affirmation, so if you do it, be prepared for changes if you are not in the appropriate career.) Babaji always taught us that work is *worship.* It helps so much to see it that way. If you can't see it that way, perhaps you should look at how you can emphasize the service aspect of your career more, or perhaps you should consider changing to a career that brings more direct service to mankind.

George Bernard Shaw said, "This is the true joy of life: To be used for a purpose recognized by yourself as a mighty one."

What is a mighty purpose to you? How do you see yourself in relationship to the world? We have an obvious spiritual obligation to others and to the planet. Begin to appreciate your connection with everyone and everything and use your career as a way of serving and expressing the joy of this connection.

CHAPTER 6
WHAT A *COURSE* IN *MIRACLES* SAYS ABOUT JOY

What does a *A Course in Miracles* say about Joy? Quite frankly, that is truly what the entire *Course* is about—how to experience Joy.

As an exercise, however, I pulled out nearly every paragraph from the *Text* that contained the word Joy, then selected the most pertinent for inclusion in this book. These excerpts, although out of context, will certainly give you an understanding of some of the main points of the *Course*. This is a great deal to digest, to be sure, so I suggest that you read it through once and then come back later and reread it again and again—one or two paragraphs at a time, allowing yourself the time to reflect and meditate carefully.

Joy is the inevitable result of gentleness. Gentleness means that fear is now impossible, and what could come to interfere with joy? The open hands of gentleness are always filled. The gentle have no pain. They cannot suffer. Why would they not be joyous? They are sure they are beloved and must be safe. Joy goes with gentleness as surely as grief attends attack. God's teachers trust in Him. And they are sure His Teacher goes before them, making sure no harm can come to them. They hold His gifts and follow in His way, because God's Voice directs them in all things. Joy is their song of thanks. And Christ looks down on them in thanks as well. His need of them is just as great as theirs of Him. How joyous it is to share the purpose of salvation!

> —Course in Miracles,
> *Teacher's Manual, Page 8,*
> *from "What Are the Charac-*
> *teristics of God's Teachers?"*

LIVING IS JOY, but death can only weep. You see in death escape from what you made. But this you do not see; that you made death, and it is but illusion of an end. Death cannot be escape, because it is not life in which the problem lies. Life has no opposite, for it is God.

> —Course in Miracles,
> *Teacher's Manual, Page 50,*
> *from "What Is the Peace of*
> *God?"*

There is one thought in particular that should be remembered throughout the day. It is a thought of pure joy: a thought of peace, a thought of limitless release, limitless because all things are freed within it.

> —Course in Miracles,
> *Teacher's Manual, Page 39*

You will understand peace and Joy when you have become willing to hide nothing. (p. 8)

All real pleasure comes from doing God's Will. (p. 12)

The ego is AFRAID OF SPIRIT'S JOY, because once you have experienced it, you will withdraw all protection from the ego, and become totally without investment in fear. (p. 50)

When your mood tells you that you have chosen wrongly, and this is so whenever you are not joyous, then know this need not be. (p. 57)

I am teaching you to associate misery with the ego and Joy with the Spirit. You have taught yourself the opposite. You are still free to choose, but can you really want the rewards of the ego in the presence of the rewards of God? (p. 62)

God, Who encompasses all being, created beings who have everything individually, but who want to share it to increase their Joy. Nothing real can be increased except by sharing. That is why God created you. Divine abstraction takes Joy in sharing. God has kept your kingdom for you, but He cannot share His Joy with you until you know it with your whole mind. (p. 64)

The Bible repeatedly states that you should praise God. God is praised whenever any mind learns to be wholly helpful. (This is impossible without being totally harmless.) The truly helpful are invulnerable because they are not protecting their egos. Their helpfulness is their praise of God. God goes out to them and through them, and there is great JOY throughout the kingdom. Every mind that is changed adds to this JOY with its individual willingness to share in it. The truly helpful are God's miracle workers, whom I direct until we are all united in the JOY of the Kingdom. (p. 65)

To heal is to make happy. I have told you to think how many opportunities you have had to gladden yourself, and how many you have refused. This is the same as telling you you have refused to heal yourself. The light that belongs to you is the light of JOY. Radiance is not associated with sorrow. JOY calls forth an integrated willingness to share it. There is no difference between love and joy. Therefore, the only possible whole state is the wholly JOYOUS. To heal or to make JOYOUS is therefore the same as to integrate and make one. (p. 66)

The Holy Spirit is the spirit of JOY. He is the call to return with which God blessed the minds of His separated Sons. The principle of Atonement and the separation began at the same time. When the ego was made, God placed in the mind the healing, the call to JOY. This call is so strong that the ego always dissolves at its sound. That is why you must choose to hear one of the two voices within you. One you made yourself and that one is not of God. But the other is given to you by God . . . Who asks you only to listen to it. (p. 69)

Whatever you accept into your mind has reality for you. I said before that you must learn to think with God. To think with Him is to think like Him. This engenders JOY, not guilt, because it is natural. Guilt is a sure sign that your thinking is unnatural.

Guilt feelings induce fears of retaliation or abandonment, and thus ensure that the future will be like the past. God offers you the continuity of eternity in exchange. When you choose to make this exchange, you will simultaneously exchange guilt for JOY . . . viciousness for love, and pain for peace. (p. 79)

Whenever you are not wholly JOYOUS, it is because you have reacted with a lack of love to one of God's creations. Perceiving this as "sin" you become defensive because you expect attack. The decision to react in this way is yours, and can therefore be undone . . . Decision cannot be difficult. This is obvious, if you realize that you must already have decided not to be wholly JOYOUS if that is how you feel. Therefore, the first step in the undoing is to recognize that you actively decided wrongly, but can actively decide otherwise. (p. 82 and 83)

A wise teacher teaches through approach not avoidance. He does not emphasize what you must avoid to escape from harm, but what you need to learn to have JOY. The Holy Spirit says:
1. To have, Give all to all.
2. To have Peace, Teach Peace to learn it.
3. Be vigilant only for God and His Kingdom.
(p. 96-103)

What you believe you are, determines your gifts, and if God created you by extending Himself as you, you can only extend yourself as He did. Only JOY increases forever, since JOY and eternity are inseparable. Eternity is the indelible stamp of the creation. The eternal are in peace and JOY forever. To think like God is to share His certainty of what you are, and to create like Him is to share the perfect Love He shares with you. To this the Holy Spirit leads you, that your JOY may be complete because the Kingdom of God is Whole. (p. 105)

Allowing insanity to enter your mind means that you have not judged sanity as wholly desirable. In this depressing state the Holy Spirit reminds you gently that you are sad because you are not fulfilling your function as co-creator with God, and are therefore depriving yourself of JOY. (p. 117)

The ego's whole thought system causes tension, and thus blocks your only function. It therefore blocks your JOY, so that you perceive yourself as unfulfilled. You do not know your JOY because you do not know your own Self-fullness. Exclude any part of the Kingdom from Yourself and you are not whole. (p. 123)

The Holy Spirit will direct you only so as to avoid pain. Surely no one would object to this goal if he recognized it. You no more recognize what is painful than you know what is JOY-FUL. You are, in fact, very apt to confuse the two. The Holy Spirit's main function is to teach you to tell them apart. What is JOYFUL to you is painful to the ego, and as long as you are in doubt about what you are, you will be confused about joy and pain. This confusion is the cause of the whole idea of sacrifice. Obey the Holy Spirit and you will be giving up the ego. (p. 124)

The Holy Spirit will always guide you truly, because your JOY is His. This is His Will for everyone because He speaks for the Kingdom of God, which IS JOY. Following Him is therefore the easiest thing in the world, and the only thing that is easy. A Son of God is happy only when he knows he is with God. (p. 126)

To fulfill the Will of God perfectly is the only JOY and peace that can be fully known, because it is the only function that can be fully experienced. Yet the wish for other experience will block its accomplishment, because God's will cannot be forced upon you, being an experience of total willingness. (p. 131)

If God's Will for you is complete peace and JOY, unless you experience only this you must be refusing to acknowledge His Will. When you are not at peace and not in JOY, it can only be because you do not believe you are in Him. Yet He is ALL in ALL. (p. 133)

No one created by God can find JOY in anything except the eternal; not because he is deprived of anything else, but because nothing else is worthy of him. What God and His Sons create is eternal, and in this and this only is their JOY. (p. 138)

The Holy Spirit's curriculum is never depressing, because it is a curriculum of JOY. Whenever the reaction to learning is depression, it is because the true goal of the curriculum has been lost sight of. (p. 141)

How can you become increasingly aware of the Holy Spirit in you except by His effects? You cannot see Him with your eyes or hear Him with your ears. How then can you perceive Him at all?? If you inspire JOY and others react to you with JOY, even though you are not experiencing JOY yourself, there must be something in you that is capable of producing it. It seems to you that the Holy Spirit does not produce JOY consistently in you only because you do not consistently arouse JOY in others. Their reactions to you are your evaluations of His consistency. When you are inconsistent you will not always give rise to JOY, and so therefore you will not always recognize HIS consistency. (p. 162)

Every minute and every second gives you a chance to save yourself. Do not lose these chances, not because they will not return, but because delay of JOY—is needless. God wills you perfect happiness NOW! (p. 163)

Do not forget, however, that to deny God will inevitably result in projection, and you will believe that others and not yourself have done this to you. You may believe that you judge your brothers by the messages they give you, but you have judged them by the message you give to them. Do not attribute your denial of JOY to them, or you cannot see the spark in them that would bring JOY to you. It is the denial of the spark that brings depression, for whenever you see your brothers without it, you are denying God. (p. 176)

O my child, if you knew what God wills for you your JOY would be complete!!!!! When you have said, "God's Will is Mine," you will see such beauty that you will know it is not of you. Out of your JOY you will create beauty in His Name, for your JOY could no more be contained than His. The bleak little world will vanish into nothingness, and your heart will be so filled with JOY that it will leap into Heaven and into the Presence of God. The way is not hard but it is very different. (p. 185)

Resurrection must compel your allegiance gladly because it is the symbol of JOY. Its whole compelling power lies in the fact that it represents what you want to be. The freedom to leave behind everything that hurts you and frightens you cannot be thrust upon you, but it can be offered you through the Grace of God. (p. 193)

Only when you see you are guiltless will you be happy. As long as you believe the Son of God is guilty you will walk along the carpet, believing it leads to death. And the journey will seem long and cruel and senseless, for so it is. The journey the Son of God has set himself is useless indeed, but the journey on which his Father sets him is one of release and JOY. You will see as you learn the Son of God is guiltless. When you have accepted the Atonement for yourself, you will realize there is no guilt in God's Son. (p. 222)

You will first dream of peace, and then awaken to it. Your first exchange of what you made for what you want is the exchange of nightmares for happy dreams of love. Love waits on welcome, and the real world is but your welcome of what always was. Therefore, the call of JOY is in it. (p. 238)

When you have learned how to decide with God, all decision becomes as easy and as right as breathing. There is no effort and you will be led as gently as if you were being carried down a quiet path in summer. The Holy Spirit will not delay in answering your every question what to do. He knows and He will tell you. How can you decide what you should do when you have already decided against your function? Remove the awful burden you have laid upon yourself by loving not the Son of God, and trying to teach him guilt instead of love. Give up this frantic and insane attempt that cheats you of the JOY OF LIVING with your God and Father. (p. 261)

God's plan for your awaking is as perfect as yours is fallible. You know not what you do, but He Who knows is with you. He would teach you nothing except how to be happy. Blessed Son of a wholly blessing Father. JOY was created for you. Your calling here is to devote yourself with active willingness, to the denial of guilt in all its forms. The inheritance of the Kingdom is the right of God's Son, given him in his creation. (p. 262)

Peace, then be unto everyone who becomes a teacher of peace. For peace is the acknowledgement of perfect purity, from which no one is excluded. Within its holy circle is everyone whom God created as His Son. JOY is its unifying attribute, with no one left outside to suffer guilt alone. The power of God draws everyone to its safe embrace of love and union. (p. 263)

The Holy Spirit teaches thus: There is no hell. Hell is only what the ego has made of the present. The Holy Spirit would undo all of this now. Fear is not of the present, but only the past and future, which do not exist. There is no fear in the present when each instant stands clear and separated from the past without its shadow reaching out into the future. Each instant is a clean, untarnished birth, and the present extends forever. It is so beautiful and so clean and free of guilt that nothing but happiness is there. No darkness is remembered and immortality and JOY are now! (p. 282)

Do not be concerned with time, and fear not the instant of holiness that will remove all fear. For the instant of peace is eternal. It will come, being the lesson God gives you, through the Teacher He has appointed to translate time into eternity. Blessed is God's Teacher, Whose JOY it is to teach God's Holy Son his holiness. His JOY is not contained in time. His teaching is for you because his JOY is yours! Through Him you stand before God's altar, where He gently translates hell into Heaven. (p. 284)

I asked you earlier, "Would you be hostage to the ego or host to God?" Let this question be asked you by the Holy Spirit every time you make a decision. For every decision you make does answer this, and invites sorrow or JOY accordingly. Every decision you make is for Heaven or for hell, and brings you the awareness (now) or what you asked for. (p. 286)

Let no despair darken the JOY of Christmas, for the time of Christ is meaningless apart from JOY. Let us join in celebratng peace by demanding no sacrifice of anyone, for so you offer me the love I offer you. What can be more JOYOUS than to perceive we are deprived of nothing?

Such is the message of the time of Christ . . . This is the time in which a new year will soon be born from the time of Christ . . . Nothing will be lacking . . . say then to your brother: "I give you to the Holy Spirit as part of myself. I know that you will be released, unless I want to use you to imprison myself. In the name of freedom I choose your release. Because I recognize that we will be released together." So will the year begin in JOY and freedom. (p. 306)

This is the Year of JOY, in which your listening will increase and peace will grow. The power of holiness and the weakness of attack are both being brought into your awareness. Remember that whenever you listened to His interpretation the results have brought you JOY. Would you prefer the results of your interpretation, considering honestly what they have been? God wills you better. (p. 310)

The Holy Relationship is learned. It is the old, unholy relationship, transformed and seen anew . . . The only difficult phase is in the beginning. For here, the goal of the relationship is abruptly shifted to the exact opposite of what it was. This is the first result of offering the relationship to the Holy Spirit for His purposes . . . The temptation of the ego becomes extremely intense with this shift of goals . . . Only a radical shift in purpose could induce a complete change of mind about what the whole relationship is for. As this change develops and is finally accomplished, it grows increasingly beneficent and JOYOUS. But at the beginning, the situation is experienced as very precarious . . . This is the time for FAITH. (p. 337-338)

I said before that the first change, before dreams disappear, is that your dreams of fear are changed to happy dreams. That is what the Holy Spirit does in the special relationship. He does not destroy it, nor snatch it away from you. The special relationship will remain, not as a source of pain and guilt, but as a source of JOY and freedom. It will not be for you alone, for therein lay its misery. (p. 351)

When you feel the holiness of your relationship is threatened by anything, stop instantly and offer the Holy Spirit your willingness, in spite of fear, to let Him exchange this instant for the holy one that you would rather have. He will never fail in this . . . It will become the happy dream through which He can spread JOY to thousands on thousands who believe that love is fear, not happiness. Let Him fulfill the function that He gave to your relationship by accepting it for you, and nothing will be wanting that would make of it what He would have it be. (p. 358)

Do you not want to know your own Identity? Would you not happily exchange your doubts for certainty? Would you not willingly be free of misery and learn again of JOY? Your holy relationship offers all this to you . . . All this is given you who would but see your brother as sinless . . . Peace will come to all who ask for it with real desire and sincerity of purpose, shared with the Holy Spirit and at one with Him on what salvation is. Be willing, then, to see your brother sinless, that Christ may rise before your vision and give you JOY. (p. 412)

There is no need to learn through pain. *And gentle lessons are acquired JOYOUSLY, and are remembered gladly. What gives you happiness you want to learn and not forget . . . Your question is whether the means by which this course is learned will bring you the JOY it promises. If you believed it would, the learning of it would be no problem. (p. 416)*

We have repeated how little is asked of you to learn this course. It is the same small willingness you need to have your whole relationship transformed to YOU; the little gift you offer to the Holy Spirit for which He gives you everything; the very little on which salvation rests; the tiny change of mind by which the crucifixion is changed to resurrection . . . This is the only thing you need do for vision, happiness, release from pain and the complete escape from sin. Say only this:

> *"I AM responsible for what I see.*
> *I choose the feelings I experience, and decide*
> *upon the goal I would achieve.*
> *And everything that seems to happen to me*
> *I ask for, and receive as I have asked." (p. 418)*

Happiness must be constant, because it is attained by giving up the wish for the inconstant. JOY cannot be perceived except through constant vision. And constant vision can be given only those who wish for constancy . . . Happiness is constant, so then you need ask for it but once to have it always. And if you do not have it always, being what it is, you did not ask for it. (p. 433-434)

Truth is the opposite of illusions because it offers JOY. What else but JOY could be the opposite of misery? To leave one kind of misery and seek another is hardly an escape. To change illusions is to make no change. The search for JOY in misery is senseless, for how could JOY be found in misery? . . . Illusions carry only guilt and suffering, sickness and death to their believers. The form in which they are accepted is irrelevant.

No form of misery in reason's eyes can be confused with JOY. JOY is Eternal. You can be sure indeed that any seeming happiness that does not last is really fear. JOY does not turn to sorrow, for the eternal cannot change. But sorrow can be turned to JOY . . . Reason will tell you that the only way to escape from misery is to recognize it and go the other way! (p. 439)

What is dependable except God's love? And where does sanity abide except in Him? The One Who speaks for Him (The Holy Spirit) can show you this, in the alternative He chose especially for you. It is God's Will that you remember this, and so emerge from deepest mourning into perfect JOY. (p. 496)

The tiny spot you see as sin that stands between you still is holding back the happy opening of Heaven's Gate. How little is the hindrance that withholds the wealth of Heaven from you. And how great will be the JOY in Heaven when you join the mighty chorus to the Love of God. (p. 511)

Swear not to die, you holy Son of God! The Son of Life cannot be killed. He is immortal as his Father. You were not born to die. (p. 572) Life's function cannot be to die. This world will bind your feet and tie your hands and kill your body ONLY if you think that it was made to crucify God's Son. For even though it was a dream of death, you need not let it stand for this to you. Let this be changed. How lovely is the world whose purpose is forgiveness of God's Son! How free from fear, how filled with blessing and with happiness, and what a JOYOUS thing it is to dwell in such a happy place. (p. 573)

It must be clear that it is easier to have a happy day if you prevent unhappiness from entering at all! But this takes practicing the rules that will protect you from the ravages of fear. The outlook starts with this:

1. "Today I will make no decisions by myself."
2. Decide how you want to feel, the kind of day you want and the things you want to happen and then say:

"If I make no decisions by myself, this is the day that will be given to me."

3. *If something happens that you did not want, say, "I hope I have been wrong," and then, "I must have decided wrongly on my own."*
4. *"I want another way to look at this." "What can I lose by asking?" (There must be lack of opposition to being helped.) (p. 583)*

CHAPTER 7

ETERNALITY

Immortality The Joy of Living and Living and Living . . .

Theodore Toethke said, "Being, not doing, is my first *Joy*." This is something to think about. Obviously, if you experience joy in being, you will probably also experience joy in doing. Do you experience joy in merely being a Being? Are you joyously glad to be alive? Do you have a burning passion for life itself? If you cannot answer yes to both of those questions, then you probably won't be interested in Physical Immortality.

But chances are that if you did discover how to feel good, have fun all the time, stay healthy and young, have what you want all the time, and live in perfection and great relationships, then you might want to stick around, and you might be extremely thankful to God for Life Itself. The trick here—the "catch-22"—is that the way to experience all of the above is to have gratitude for life to such a degree that you want to live forever and choose that constantly.

I have written on the subject of Physical Immortality in my book *Rebirthing in the New Age*. I have listed other books on the subject in the back of all my books. And for this book, I decided to share with you what *A Course in Miracles* says on the subjects of life and death:

Death is not your Father's Will nor yours. The death penalty is the ego's ultimate goal, for it truly believes that you are a criminal deserving of death. The death penalty never leaves the ego's mind; for that is what it always reserves for you in the end. It will torment you while you live; but its hatred is not satisfied until you die. As long as you feel guilty you are listening to the Voice of the ego, which tells you that you have been treacherous to God and therefore deserve death.

You will think that death comes from God and not from the ego, because by confusing yourself with the ego, you believe that you want death! When you are tempted to the desire for death, remember that I *did not die! Would I have overcome death for myself alone? And would eternal life have been given to one of the Father's sons unless He had also given it to you? When you learn to make me manifest, you will never see death.*

The acceptance of guilt into the mind of God's son was the beginning of the separation. The world you see is a delusional system of those made mad by guilt. This is so because the world is a symbol of punishment and all the laws that seem to govern it are the laws of death. The ego's path is sorrow/separation/death. If this were the real world, God would be cruel!

Love (God) does not kill to save. Your will to live is blocked by the capricious and unholy whim of death and murder that your Father does NOT share with you.

Each day, each hour and minute and every second, you are deciding between the crucifixion and the resurrection . . . between the ego and the Holy Spirit. Crucifixion is always the ego's aim.

Nothing is accomplished through death. Everything is accomplished through life *and life is of the mind and in the mind. If we share the same mind, you can overcome death because I did!!*

Death is an attempt to resolve conflict by not deciding at all. Like any other solution the ego attempts, IT WILL NOT WORK. To the ego, the Goal is death. The ego is insane. (p. 280 & 359)

Heaven is not a place or a condition. It is merely an awareness of perfect Oneness.

Error is different than sin. If sin were possible, it would be irreversible. It calls for punishment. Error merely calls for correction. Sin is not real. Sin is the grand-illusion underlying all the ego's grandiosity. For by it, God Himself would be changed and rendered incomplete. This is arrogance. The Son of God can be mistaken, but he cannot sin. There is nothing he can do to change his true reality.

But to the ego, purity is seen as arrogance and the acceptance of the self as sinful is perceived as holiness. The ego demands punishment (death) for its "sin." And yet, if sin is real, God must be at war with Himself. If sin is real, both God and you are not real.

To the ego, sin means death, so atonement is achieved through murder. Salvation is looked upon as a way by which the Son of God was killed instead of you (Jesus). Yet, no one can die for anyone and death does not atone for sin.

To you and your brother, it is given to release and be released from the dedication to death.

*No one can die unless he chooses death (all death is therefore suicide). What seems to be the fear of death is really its attraction.

***Death is the result of the thought we call the ego, (i.e., "Death is inevitable"), as surely as life is the result of the thought of God.

From the ego came sin and guilt and death in opposition to life and innocence. The Will of God, who created neither sin nor death, wills not that you be bound by them. The shrouded figures in the funeral procession, march not in honor of their Creator. They are NOT following his Will, they are opposing it.

THE MESSAGE OF THE CRUCIFIXION

There is a positive interpretation of the crucifixion that is devoid of fear, and therefore, if properly understood, benign in what it teaches.

The crucifixion did not establish the Atonement; the Resurrection did. Many sincere Christians have misunderstood this . . . No one who is free of the belief in scarcity could possibly make this mistake. If the crucifixion is seen from an upside-down point of view, it does appear as if God permitted, and even encouraged one of His Sons to Suffer because he was good. This particularly unfortunate interpretation arose out of projection and has led many people to be bitterly afraid of God. Such anti-religious concepts enter into many religions. Yet the real Christian should pause and ask, "How could this be?" (p. 84)

Is it likely that God Himself would be capable of this kind of thinking which in His Own Words have clearly stated is unworthy of His Son?

The Resurrection demonstrated that nothing can destroy truth: God can withstand any form of evil as light abolishes forms of darkness.

The crucifixion is nothing more than an extreme teaching device. Its value, like the value of any teaching device, lies solely in the kind of learning it facilitates.

It can and has been misunderstood. This is because the fearful are apt to perceive fearfully. The crucifixion represents release from fear to anyone who understands it. The message the crucifixion was intended to teach is that it is not necessary to perceive any form of assault in persecution, because you cannot be persecuted.

When you are tempted to yield to the desire for death, remember that I did not die. Would I have overcome death for myself

80

alone? I have said that the crucifixion is the symbol of the ego. When it was confronted with the real guiltlessness of God's Son, it did attempt to kill him and the reason it gave was the guiltlessness is blasphemous to God. To the ego, the ego is God, and guiltlessness must be interpreted as the final guilt that fully justifies murder!

Easter is the sign of peace, not pain. This week we celebrate life (Resurrection), not death. We cannot be united in crucifixion and death. The time of Easter is the time for JOY. (pages 84, 92, 217, 224, 396)

THE JOY OF MEETING OTHER IMMORTALISTS

In our community we share the excitement of learning to master physical immortality together. Every once in a while we are privileged to have the thrill of finding a true immortalist, who came to this truth on his own in another interesting way. When this happens, it is like discovering a gem. Words can hardly express the feeling of joy and relief. There is an instant rapport and intimacy. There is an instant connection of wanting to serve together. It is either "Let's get to work" or "How can we work together right away?" or "How can I support your work more right now?" There is a natural desire to be together as much as possible. That may not be logistically possible, since most immortalists are spread out around the globe, or they travel constantly. But there is a passion to work it out so the paths cross as often as possible.

There is a pervasive sense of wellbeing among Immortalists—a vibration that is unbeatable. It is ecstasy—and it doesn't even have to be talked about. I thought it would be appropriate to share a recent experience I had when I met Robert Coon. It is my supreme joy and honor to introduce him into your life.

MY PURE JOY OF KNOWING A FELLOW IMMORTALIST I would like to share the joy of one of deep immortal friendships, as I am sure you will be delighted to find out about the presence of the great Immortal Poet, Robert Coon, who is currently living in Glastonbury.

In 1985 we had the privilege of doing the LRT Spiritual Retreat in Glastonbury, England. Imagine the wonderful surprise of being greeted with a letter, upon arrival, such as the one I'm sharing with you below:

AN IMMORTALIST WELCOME TO GLASTONBURY *The most radical act is also the most loving act. The most loving act is the most anarchistic and subversive act. This most loving is the overcoming of death, the attainment of Physical Immortality—and the global communication and sharing of your attainment.*

The battle against death must be fought on every front. We begin by overcoming deathist thoughts, words and deeds in our own life. Then we must root out the fabric of decay from relationships and from social structures throughout the world.

One such deathist social structure is orthodox religion. At the recent Glastonbury Pilgrimmage conducted by the Church of England, such anti-Christ sentiments as "Glorify God by your death" and "God in his mercy brings you an early death" were expressed by church leaders. These ideas are obscene.

The Christ truth is this: You betray God's gift to you by allowing yourself to die. To glorify God means to exalt the atoms and cells of your own physical body into a purified instrument of Divine Will and Spirit. And the greatest mercy God may show is the near illumination of the Way to Physical Immortality—a Way which is unique and individual for every being. We use the term "Physical Immortality" rather than Eternal Life, so that there can be no excuse for failing to understand what we are talking about.

Many pilgrims journey to Glastonbury to examine its past. I believe that You who read these words have come here to contribute to the Living Presence and Immortalist Future of Glastonbury. We have much to learn and much to share with each other here at the "Heart Chakra of the World."

For Glastonbury is the heart center of this earth. It is from here that the truth of Immortality is being fully revealed to the world. This is the deepest secret of the Holy Grail. To win the Grail is to overcome death and obtain Immortal Life. To chain the Grail to a lesser, more easily obtainable goal is a limitation of vision and is ignoble and unworthy of the Divine Potential of the Human Spirit.

If the force and enthusiasm needed to communicate this Truth of Immortality to the world are dependent upon a physical manifestation, then—God willing—may that physical manifestation occur Now. Of if belief and the ability to hear this Truth suffice by themselves, then today is the appointed time.

The Word is being made Flesh through Glastonbury. An International Immortalist gathering such as this is an ideal vehicle for the birthing of the Truth of Physical Immortality to the world. The Immortals of the Glastonbury Shamballic Focus bid thee welcome to Glastonbury—Ancient Avalon and New Jerusalem. May this "God Training" be the first of many such Immortalist gatherings here at the Grail and heart center of this living planet Gaea.

I charge each of you to share this message with all beings as rapidly as Love allows. May you leave Glastonbury charged with the Spirit of Life Eternal in every atom of your being and filled to overflowing with the desire to overcome all things!

—Robert Coon
July 1, 1985

I had never met Robert, and I was looking forward to it, but I certainly did not expect it to happen as it did. I was told that I should consider taking my group to the top of the Tor at midnight (the night before the retreat began). I was told there were going to be ceremonies. Since it was raining, and the training had not really started, I made it optional. About half the group trekked up the mountain with Fredric, my co-trainer, and me. We crossed cow pastures and climbed fences. It was dark and windy. I certainly did not imagine Robert would be up there, and was I ever surprised when suddenly a man appeared who looked like he was from a different era, who captured absolutely everyone's attention immediately, so much so that my students begged him to go on and on even though the rain fell more and more. We were all spellbound by this man's presence and his most alluring "Invocations to Immortalists"—which none of us were expecting to hear at all. "Could he have actually written those poetic words himself?" I wondered. "Could anyone on this plane actually write that?" I asked myself. I finally ran to him, kissed him, and said, "You are my brother. Please come teach my class."

Here are three beautiful poems by Robert Coon that I would like to share with you:

Easter Everywhere

Unseal the Heart and Mind of every Star with this melody of
   Perfect truth singing from the temple of your soul . . . Proclaim
Our Word of light made flesh in all beings and speak forth
The laws of heaven forevermore. You are the final
Resurrection of this world, born from my womb of infinite
Joy; and I am your Bride, garlanded with a halo of all the
Prayers of love and peace that have been and shall ever be!

Radiate this song with all thy lust of spirit and every nation
   Shall be lifted up and quickened by our love . . . Praise all
Things and all times throughout Eternity and flames of divine
Perfection will engulf and illuminate this universe. We
Gave birth to this reality so that all stars might have
Incorruptible bodies—Holy temples with which to praise one
Another in total harmony with Divine Will! Create every
Thought, word and deed with the same alchemy of wisdom and
Perfect relationship and death shall never touch thee . . .

84

Rejoice in the day when every Star sees clearly the river
   Of its light shining through every life and sees only the
   Alpha and everchanging Omega of Divine Perfection—for that
   Great Day Is At Hand . . . Shout your holy word from every shrine
   On earth from Shasta to Glastonbury and your prayers shall
   Be glorified in their power. Invoke angels and deities of
   Every land and faith to heal, awaken and vitalize the Body
   Of our mother planet! Summon all Masters from all planes
   Back to earth and may they claim their final diamond bodies . . .

You are God . . . Emanate all your energy and Will through this Rose
   Of your heart in a mighty threefold symphony of Praise, Love
   And Gratitude for all things without exception and ye shall
   Ignite our Grail of Immortality and transfiguration within
   The soul of every atom of every God. Heed this song with
   All your Faith and all your strength and 'tis certain
   Ye shall be raised from mortality and uplifted into the
   Vibration of a translated being of Light and Total Freedom
   To come and go at the speed of love as ye Will in the Body
   Of Christ! These Works and Greater do I command and
   Promise thee for every woman and every man and every being
   Is a Star!

—Robert Coon

FIRST SUPPER

Children of Earth! Feast upon these Fruits of eternal
   Majesty plucked from the Tree of Life as all your
   Highest dreams converge in a mighty vortex to devour
   This Universe in a whirlwind of compassionate frenzy
   May this Rising Sun pierce your hearts with swords
   Of perfect love dipped in the most sweet venom of
   Sacred Truth!

Drink this chalice of jeweled nectar distilled from
   Orgasms of Stars and know that Ye are Goddesses and
   Gods ravished with Joy far beyond realms of birth
   and death. Your bodies shall be angels of light for
   Behold! Ye shall dare to make All things new with
   This immaculate love we conceive endless Milleniums!

Now come and go as the Wind and bathe all eternity
   With mighty torrents of love, praise and gratitude
   As we enrapture this planet to the very core
   Forever and evermore I hear this paradise singing
   Joyous prayers lofted high thrue Raindow dew magic
   Incense of our previous being returns to its womb
   Made fruitful and multiplied by alchemy of these
   Words I still hear you saying Oh Let There Be Light!

And if an Angel should appear please bid it stay awhile
   And be Thy Lover! Dedicate your passion to the
   Highest and let us always greet one another in this
   Garden of the heart of Love made glorious with
   Total Perfection of the Will Divine!

—Robert Coon

EAGLE GIFTS OF IMMORTALITY

Angel of Revelation! Blaze forth upon Star lanes
   Embraced by canopy of Nuit! Herald this final stratagem
   Of eagle sages smiling at Shamballa . . . Oh let my hymn
   Ascend onto the diadem of the new born Phoenix
   For I have fathomed the cypher of thy Play!

Fly on thrue limitless caverns of Buddha Mind illuminated
   By thy passing torch of clarity and I will follow
   In your wake of vision enrobed in lightning—
My eyes ever faithful to the pole star of this voyage . . .

Hold fast thy ankh of immortality as we run upon a boulevard
  From Saturn to the Sun—for we have seized the reins
  Of Life from death and drive the chariot of the Grail
  Into the Holy Kingdom of the City of the Pyramids and beyond!

Serpentine fibers of thy love twine about my heart and guide me
  To the roots of the Tree of Life . . . My path is clear!
  This—the hour of transmutation spoken of in perfect
  Silence at the foundation of this world . . . I write this
  Sacred oath of alchemy upon a golden scroll:
  I shall nourish these roots with laughter of Stars
  And Praise of Saint until a Fruit never known
  Before in All Creation anoints the tongue of every being
  Nesting in this Tree of Aspiration with a taste
  Regenerating Paradise!

Now place the capstone of thy Will upon the Summit
  Of the Great Pyramid . . . All prophecies are fulfilled!
  Reveal to all the glorious destiny of our planet!
  May every Star assume the rightful Mastery
  Of its own realm! Open this gift and show me
  Thy eternal Godhood!

—Robert Coon

A selection of Robert Coon's prose, essays, prophesies, and poetic invocations concerning the global unfoldment of Physical Immortality have recently been published in a special numbered edition by Griffin Gold Publications. Copies are available, signed, with Immortalist Blessing, and the title is: *VOYAGE TO AVALON: An Immortalist's Introduction to the Magick of Glastonbury.* This book is available directly from Robert Coon, 20 Selwood Road, Glastonbury, Somerset, England. Order by sending checque, cash, or postal order to Robert Coon in $8.00 U.S. or 5.5 pounds U.K.

CHAPTER 8

OTHER WAYS OF LOVING GOD

Essays by Loving Relationships Trainers

PURE LOVE

by Bob Mandel

Nothing approaches love in its ability to purify you. If you want to be pure, find someone you love and let him, or her, love the hell out of you! That's what I did with my wife Mallie. I had tried many spiritual disciplines over the years—yoga, meditation, fasting, silence, chanting, EST, rebirthing, you name it! And each technique proved valuable in its own way. But until I met Mallie and surrendered to loving and being loved fully, I never experienced the purity of my own essence.

Love alone is the ultimate purification process because love alone is absolutely pure. It cannot tolerate impurity, sickness, negativity of any sort, and brings up anything unlike itself for the purpose of release. There is no love but the love of God because when you are in love you are in a state of deep gratitude for all of creation. The feeling of utter perfection in your heart opens your eyes to all that God has give you. When you surrender to love, you emerge from behind your ego and experience your Oneness and holiness.

Spiritual disciplines can be an extremely valuable part of the process of surrender. In committing oneself to such disciplines, the ego is confronted by a simple, spiritual ritual. For example, silence confronts the noise of your mind, fasting confronts your addiction to food, breathing confronts your addiction to lifelessness. In order to experience pure joy, however, one must go beyond the discipline to the love. As such, spiritual discipline is a wonderful vehicle, but it should not be mistaken for the destination itself. You can lead a horse to water, but drinking the divine is an act of personal choice and surrender.

The appropriate attitude towards discipline, or technique, is not that hard work produces results, but rather that joyful work is a celebration of gratitude. If the path is unhappy, the end of the journey is not likely to be any happier. In each step of the quest you are faced with the same ultimate choice: to surrender to love and joy or to resist and create struggle and pain. In surrendering, you are blessed in the Holy Instant: in resisting you simply postpone your inevitable awakening.

The reason so many people are spiritual "junkies," chasing each new spiritual fad compulsively, is that they reach the same point of no return with each new discipline. And that is the point of surrender. The point of yielding to God's love. The point of transformation. If one is unwilling to let go, each new path quickly turns into a dead end. In the long run, the path is only as righteous as the traveler. And a traveler with a light heart, a heart full of love, will always find the light at the end of the tunnel because, in a sense, he has already chosen that Light. Heaven is a choice one must make, and continue to make each step of the way.

All too often, spiritual seekers are stuck in a struggle pattern. They have transferred the struggle for worldly goods to the struggle for heavenly riches. Moreover, they tend to use their enlightenment to beat themselves up for their imperfection, rather than forgive themselves, learn their lessons, and surrender. They forget that the first element of enlightenment is lightening up, or not taking oneself seriously. Instead of laughing, they grunt. And they justify their pain in the name of God, somehow thinking that makes it better. But struggle is struggle, no matter what the goal. And God does not give extra credit to those who struggle for His love the most. On the contrary, those who choose peace of mind, and ease and pleasure in the body, seem to receive the spiritual treasures instantaneously, while the strugglers seem to wrestle with the truth as though it were the angel of Death. The joy is there for the having, here and now, not there and then.

The first choice required is pure love of oneself, i.e. unconditional acceptance and respect for yourself under all circumstance. This can seem like a huge sacrifice, but the only things being sacrificed are your guilt, punishment, and separation. Yes, in order to forgive yourself completely and surrender to your own true essence, you must relinquish all the little lies, all the limiting thoughts you've been hiding behind. You must confess your own magnificence, letting go of who you pretend to be and who you fear you might be. In developing such a holy relationship with yourself, you come to experience the eternal truths about yourself:

1. You are good enough just the way you are!
2. You are worthy of God's love!
3. You are innocent!
4. You are perfect!
5. You are forgiven!

And, most of all, you are already loved, and once you get your mind out of the way, pure love is all that remains!

The second choice required is the commitment to loving relationships. All too often, people love God, or say they do, but when it comes to other people, forget it! This, of course, is a contradiction since God is Everyone! God's directive to us is to love thy neighbor as oneself, and even to love thy enemy because the love of humanity *is* the love of God. In choosing to love everyone unconditionally, you accelerate the process of loving yourself unconditionally since everyone you love is a reflection of yourself. The only enemy is the enemy within, which is the part of yourself that remains unforgiven.

A one-to-one loving relationship is the ultimate truth test. The love between two individuals contains the potential for total joy and aliveness. Of course, that love will threaten the defense mechanisms of the ego more than anything. It is therefore essential to release all attack thoughts, all thoughts of mistrust and separation, in order to taste the sweet joy of a holy relationship.

The desire for a special relationship is the most subtle trick of the ego. It causes you to see your partner as a substitute for God instead of His expression. If you take your personal separation and add it to your partner's separation, you have merely found temporary shelter from a universe you perceive as cold and cruel—which is not God's universe but your ego's substitute. This path is doomed to failure because the ego will eventually divide the couples just as surely as this couple has chosen to separate itself from God.

The solution, and the third choice required, is a holy purpose, a global focus to lift the couple out of isolation, and allow the cocoon of love to blossom into the butterfly of global awareness. Global love is based on the concept that all people are created equal, in the image of God, diverse individuals, yes, but essentially part of one unifying energy. Your choice to love equal but diverse individuals is your choice to love all forms of God's energy, which is unconditional love practiced on a planetary scale. So it is essential, for ourselves as individuals as well as for the world, that we all serve the planet as a whole. The world is your own back yard, and in caring for this yard you expand yourself to experience the incredible variety of joy available.

The final mission is the creation of heaven on earth, which is not a pipedream but the only reality worth living and loving! This process occurs one by one with each new person you meet, at home, work and play. Can you allow your ego to melt and surrender to the pure love that wants to make you whole? It is all God asks of you.

The answer is not in the discipline, i.e. the vehicle, but in the driver itself. Because the driver, at his core, is pure love!

MUSIC AS AN EXPRESSION OF GOD
by Fredric Lehrman

My career as a musician had many roots. As a child I was used to hearing music in the house. My father was a self-taught mandoline player and would often practice popular melodies and light classics in the evening after my brother and I had been put to bed and were supposed to be sleeping. I always enjoyed these concerts. We also learned to sing all kinds of songs as a family, and our long drives to the country were always musical. As far back as I can remember, we had a phonograph and a large assortment of records which I came to know well.

When I was six I saw a bugle in the window of a music store and soon had learned to wake people up and summon them to dinner or to battle. The next year, I heard a boy play the accordian at school, and came home wanting to learn this apparently very effective method of impressing girls. This started my formal musical education, although I soon came to regret my choice of such a heavy instrument. I continued to drag this thing around for three years, eventually learning to play well at the intermediate level. But I was still unaware of what music really was all about.

Sometime around my ninth birthday, I was sitting at my desk doing my nightly homework. I had the radio on, and was listening as usual to the top tunes. A song came on which I didn't particularly like, so I casually turned the dial to find another popular station. By accident, I crossed the one channel which had classical music, and a sound came out of the radio which made me stop. It was a clear, high, shimmering tone, golden and alive, which seemed to float before me like a hummingbird. My mind was swept into it. The sound, which was actually a long trilling pair of notes, began to rise by slow degrees, higher and higher. After a long climb it reached the top, and then a series of smooth cascading scales flowed down and around and drew me into a trance of concentration.

I remained motionless throughout the whole piece, which turned out to be Beethoven's Violin Concerto. I had never heard an instrument sound like this. I marveled at the rightness of every note.

When the music ended I was a changed person. I felt that through this music I had been shown something in myself which had never before been articulated. At nine years old, my mind was filled with new possibilities. I was inspired to seek this excellence in all aspects of life.

In the years since that discovery I have followed the path of art outwards into the world and inwards into myself. Eventually both directions lead to the same place, a state of being present.

I think that the finest expression is that which lets an impulse, an energy, or a perception come through unmuted, just as it is, but with a quality of caring wrapped around it. Caring is the individual saying "I love this." It is both personal and impersonal; it is God-like; it presents and represents in the same moment. When the greatest musicians play, the successive layers of craft vanish . . . the instrument, the notes, the body and its techniques, even the compose and the theme all dissolve, leaving the listener with a direct and wordless knowing of the Universe and the Self shining through the polished crystal of art.

Art may be used for less than this. It can be used to distract, to amuse, to polemicize, to anaesthetize, to seduce. And life imitates art in these same ways. We reveal ourselves by our choices of style and by our ways of using energy. To what degree of excellence do we take our awareness?

If we are to know the purest joy we must, like God, contain and express the whole Universe. God is the ultimate artist, and reality is the highest form of art. We imitate God's function when we express our mastery. This is why we honor, adore, and reward the artists in society. When they work their craft to the point where the physical becomes transparent and smooth, they open a window into our common Godness.

If you want to know God, become an instrument. Feel your way to balance; listen deeply and find your proper tuning. Practice until the elements begin to integrate and start to come through you as if you were dreaming them, without effort. Then start again and refine it all once more. By this practice, like the alchemist's repeated distillation of the same quantity of water, you will gradually come to the attunement of inner and outer, the Philosopher's Stone which transmutes everything to gold.

Practicing music is like repeating a mantra. I let myself be reshaped by the tones I play until they cleanse me of my clumsiness, my fears, my defensive control patterns. Mechanical practice does little; for this reason I suspect that mechanical devotion does little as well. If you want to be a window for God, you must practice life with aware-ness. Pure joy involves living artfully with truth, love, simplicity, and in a mode of service. You can choose the style, but you cannot change the purpose. "Your life is God's gift to you . . . what you make of it is your gift to God." Make your life a musical offering, and God will sing with you and through you.

How to Love God Through Sex And How That Leads to Joy
by Rhonda Levand

When Sondra asked me to write a chapter for this book on how to love God through sex and how that leads to joy, I thought, that's great, and it will be easy. After all, I have spent the last 20 years exploring sexuality and what it means to be a woman. I had even committed to write a book on sex and sexuality. But, like everything else that is good for me, I put off writing this and procrastinated to the last minute. Of course, writing about God and sex will only teach me more and make me look closer at what makes me click sexually.

I really love sex. Sex is one of my favorite pleasures and always makes me happier. *A Course in Miracles*, Lesson 101 states, "God's will for me is perfect happiness." Allowing myself to love physically in the presence of another is really God's will for me because it leads me to happiness and peace of mind.

I want to backtrack a little and state that sex was not always a joy and easy for me. Through all the work I have done on myself, espe-cially Rebirthing, The Loving Relationships Training, and A Course in Miracles, sex has become the pure joy that it is supposed to be for me.

I came into this world with the implication that I would be a boy. My parents already had two daughters. They waited 10 years to try one more time for a boy. Initially at my birth, their reaction was dis-appointment. And I made the decision that I am a disappointment because I am the opposite of what my parents wanted. I am a girl, not a boy. Of course, right after my parent's initial reaction, they were thrilled with me and loved me dearly. But I carried with me the uncon-scious decision that I have to be opposite of what I am to please my

95

parents who love me. So all my life I tried to be the boy my father wanted to please him. I was athletic, tall and skinny, outgoing, and had all the characteristics a good son would have. Somewhere around the age of 13, my father was gone a lot, commuting from L.A. to Chicago, for a year. Since my father wasn't there to please, I started to get into a rebellious mode. After the age of 13, unconsciously I rebelled and was always doing the opposite of what my parents or I wanted. Coincidentally, this was also the time I started menstruating, demonstrating that I was a woman . . . not a man. I even married a man completely opposite to what I wanted in order to prove that since I am the opposite of what my parents wanted, I don't deserve what I truly want. I spent years trying to prove that I was wanted and desirable as a woman through sex. I could never be satisfied; however, I did become good at satisfying men.

After taking The Loving Relationships Training and rebirthing regularly, I started to learn to love myself completely and unconditionally as a woman. I started to celebrate and enhance my femininity. When I totally accepted that I had chosen to be a woman and rcognized the gifts I had received from my parents, my whole life took a new turn. I realized that I was a surprisingly wonderful woman. I no longer had to seek recognition from the outside that I was wanted as a woman. I knew it deep within my core. I recognized my beauty, purity, and God-self that had been sleeping inside of me.

Once I had awakened the God within me, sex took on a whole new meaning. The God within me was looking for the God within a wonderful loving man to unite with. As soon as I had accepted the God within myself, I did attract a wonderful man, Jeff Baker, who recognized that in me and in himself.

For the first time in my life, I was surrendered enough to my feminine self that I was able to receive the total joy, bliss, and that at-one feeling that you feel when you are really connected to God and the oneness of all life. Looking into the eyes of someone you love is like looking into the mirror of your own God-self.

At the same time that I was experiencing this wonderful love affair with myself and with Jeff, I had started a six-week intensive training on sex called "Lightening Up On Sex" for women only. Sondra and I had worked on the outline of the class together. I had thought the purpose of the class was to get information for the book on sex I wanted to write. Of course, it became much more than that.

Over and over again, I am learning that we teach what we need to learn. The six people in the group all became my teachers. I received tremendous gifts and perhaps got more out of the six-week experience than anyone. What we started to do was tell the complete truth about sex. Since I had so much experience with sex, I thought I was an expert, but in reality, I was just a baby. One of the truths I discovered was that I had lied about having orgasms to please the men in my life. Since in the past, I was denying my femininity, I was also denying my ability to receive joy and pleasure as a woman from a man. I went from being lucky to receive one orgasm to having multiple orgasms on a regular basis. Having an orgasm is allowing yourself to totally trust yourself and your partner.

It means to totally relax and let go in the presence of another, as you can when you masturbate. Breathing a lot helps to let in more pleasure and love. The pure joy in orgasm is allowing yourself to be totally defenseless, and completely vulnerable.

A Course in Miracles can be a textbook for sexuality. The lessons help you to strip away your defenses. The purpose of *A Course in Miracles* is to end separation and to establish atonement. Atonement means At-one-ment with God. The ultimate, physically, in being at one with your brother is the sexual union. In order to have bliss and joy in sex, we must strip all of our judgments and disapprovals away. "Forgiveness is the key to happiness." (*CIM*, Lesson 121) The more we forgive and let go of the past, the more able we are to recognize the God in ourselves and everyone else. Forgiveness is essential for living in the moment, which is God's time.

The more I strip away my defenses, judgments, and my addiction to being right, the more capable I am of truly loving myself and my neighbors, because everyone is a part of me. In the LRT we say, "Become the person you are looking for." I had to become the unconditionally loving God-Being I wanted before I could attract that into my life. One of the ways I did this was to practice celibacy for seven months. This allowed me to learn to love myself and not depend on someone else to do that for me. Instead of coming out of a need for someone to love me, I could come from a place of celebrating how wonderful I was with another person, and celebrating their uniqueness.

I am letting more and more love, joy and sex into my life. I notice there are many times I still go unconscious or asleep on my lover. There is a part of me that still doesn't want to be 100% there and into joy at every moment. I am going in that direction, however. By recognizing all that I don't want in my life, unconsciousness being one of them, I am allowing myself to create more and more of what I want.

Having pure joy means to me being grateful at every moment for all the wonderful people and experiences I have in my life, acknowledging the presence of God in my life, daily seeing the God in everyone, in the grains of sand, in the ocean, in the waves, in the sky, and seeing the oneness I have with every particle in the Universe.

Sex is a way I experience on a very physical level that at-oneness with another being. Having the feeling of all my cells uniting with all the cells of another person; feeling that person's excitement, bliss, and physical sensations running through my body.

God and Pregnancy
by Meg Kane

The first thought that comes to me in thinking about God and pregnancy is how the simple act of making love can create such a major miracle! Creating a baby may be one of the simplest and most normal acts in the world, but trying to grasp the significance, wonder and miracle of a new soul coming through your body is impossible. It is a time when mere biology cannot begin to make a *dent* in explaining what's going *on* in there; when we know God has been at work, because surely Peter and I couldn't have begun to do all this on our own.

Pregnancy is a time for returning to the source, to God, especially since you are in such a state of creating yourself! It is a time to feel close to the earth. During the spring and summer, as I felt nature more deeply, I remembered when I was young. I would keep a close eye on the trees to see when they began to bud, and then watch the leaves unfold, feeling the joy of God through nature. Pregnancy is like that; what is going on inside feels in harmony with the cherry blossoms and flowers, that life is constantly unfolding. The affirmation, "the world is my womb" feels very true to me as I feel more and more bonded to this baby, nature, God, Peter and to myself.

As I talk to this baby, I am deeply impressed with how this is not just a baby, but a unique being all of its own. I often tell "Baby Kane" it is a perfect, divine and spiritual being (it usually feels like an affirmation it already knows!). The joy that this being has taught *me* is immeasurable; as I talk to it, I find myself talking to two children sometimes, and "they" are loving me back. Being with this baby has brought me closer to God in a very real way; not only because it is such an unbelievable miracle, but because it has taught me to love in a deeper, more innocent and unconditional way. I understand the deep, unconditional love of God, and how easy it is for God to give such powerful love.

Being pregnant (I've two-and-a-half months to go as I write this) is sometimes an emotional rollercoaster that teaches me all kinds of interesting things about myself; it is also a state of grace to be a co-creator with God. It has shown me that *all* our creations, whether painting or writing or making a baby, are indeed co-creations, and by realizing this we can recognize God's joy in *all* our creations, and especially the one we are constantly co-creating with Him: ourselves!

Rebirthing as Cellular Bliss
by Peter Kane

Rebirthing is a celebration of pure joy. It is a breathing process which fills the body with oxygen and aliveness, life energy, spirit, prana, chi, and a sense of God. There have been many attempts to describe this energy. It is as varied as any life experience. Each term is limited, so I use them all, as each brings out a different quality. The name "rebirthing" is not used to imply a religious experience of being "born again," although it is often a spiritual experience because of the renewing effects of this breathing process.

Often one's separation from joy can start at birth. The effects of our first experience of life outside the womb have been well documented by studies in perinatal psychology which have appeared in the last decade. Rebirthing helps to dissolved the sense of separation at birth and puts one back in touch with the original source of joy, which is life itself.

As a physical experience, rebirthing cleanses away physical tension. The result is greater peace and aliveness physically. Life energy seems to neutralize anything which is contrary to it. The body is the storehouse of feelings. Thus, by starting with physical cleansing, rebirthing confronts mental and emotional issues in the body and provides the energy to release them with a minimum of struggle. Rebirthing is like letting God in to clean house, sweeping away the tensions, the points of separation, leaving you in touch with yourself, with joy, with aliveness, and with God.

When I began rebirthing, I was studying psychology. I was becoming disenchanted with the slowness of the methods; I was looking for something that would work faster and on a deeper level. Rebirthing got me so high that it became impossible to beat myself up. In the middle of such pure joy and alivenenss, I could not focus on the negative issues. I was home; rebirthing gave me cellular self-esteem. It was bliss, a dance of God in my body. My life began to change. I had new strength and my psychological issues began to be resolved.

I believe that personal growth comes through conscious awareness of one's issues and taking practical action to choose out of one's negatives habits. I feel it is important to practice many of the established approaches to psychological transformations. But rebirthing is one of the most blissful and has helped me invoke a spiritual energy in my life that is miraculous!

Loving God Through Meditation
by Vince Betar

When I was about 12 years old, I died, or at least seemed to. During this brief period, I remember experiencing an amazing sense of expansion, joy and unconditional love and then consciously choosing to come back into my body and live. I suppressed this experience for quite a while, yet I can see that for years it served as an unconscious motivator. On some level, part of me knew that this kind of aware-ness was supposed to be part of being alive. I had had a glimpse of another reality, of what it felt like, perhaps to "be enlightened" if only temporarily. My sense of "self" shifted radically and yet I still needed to somehow learn to ground that experience, to be able to feel that level of joy, love and expansion without leaving my body.

When I was about 16, I met an Indian Yogi visiting Sydney, was initiated into meditation, and began studying yoga. At that time I was working in the fashion industry, and my biggest passion had been surfing. I found him to be a tremendous source of inspiration and continued studying with him for the next three years. I was then introduced by some friends to Transcendental Meditation and experienced another profound shift. After a year I decided to go to Europe to train as a TM Teacher with Maharishi Mahesh Yogi. For the next eleven years I traveled throughout the world, continuing my studies and research in the field of consciousness development, estab-lishing TM Centers, teaching meditation and TM siddis and par-ticipating in advanced, long-term experimental meditation courses with Maharishi. In 1976 I was awarded a Masters Degree in Vedic Science from the Meru Institute in New Deli, India. In short, I have had a long, intimate relationship with meditation and believe that it can have a profound effect on the level of joy, love and connection that we experience in our lives.

About five years ago I discovered Rebirthing and the LRT and began a process of integrating what I had mastered inwardly via the proc-ess of Eastern meditation with Western forms of Consciousness Tech-nology. I went to America and participated in the EST Training, the EST 6-day, Insight, the LRT and a number of other courses and began an intensive training program with the LRT Institute. As I worked with rebirthing and began integrating all I was learning, it seemed that life itself became the ashram. It is interesting that it was during this time that I got married, because what was going on for me inter-nally during this time was a marriage as well. A union was going on inside me between east and west; between the inward stroke of medi-tation and receptivity and the outward stroke of action in relation-ships and the physical world.

When Yve (my wife) and I teach about relationships, we often include the idea that there is an internal relationship going on within each one of us, of which most people are unaware. We have found that our external relationships, especially our most intimate one, tends to in many ways be a reflection of our internal one.

Our inner female is our yin or receptive side. Our inner male is our yang or active side. In an ideal situation, there is a passionate and intimate relationship going on between these two internal aspects. Our yin side could be called intuition. It is our connection to the Source (to inner guidance, or spirit, or the directing intelligence of the Universe). In the ideal loving internal relationshp the yin side is open and receptive, constantly receiving inspiration, guidance, information, insight and direction and our yang side is backing it up with action and getting the job done on the physical plane.

The problem for most of us, however, is that between our intuitive aspect and our manifesting aspect we have what we call an "ego filter" that prevents or distorts real internal intimacy. Our inner aspects seem to be distanced or disconnected from each other by this set of conditioned beliefs and reactive patterns.

According to A Course in Miracles, the ego is a set of limiting, negative beliefs about ourselves and how the Universe works that we empower with our life energy. The problem with these beliefs is that they are based on mis-perceptions and false conclusions. Ultimately, they are not true, but since we are each the creators of our own experience of reality, they seem to us to be true because we believe in them and we see evidence for them reflected out in the world.

The beliefs that crystallize into what we call the ego (and this definition of ego is a bit different than the classic Freudian one) center around the illusions of separation, limitation, guilt, fear, lack, loss, struggle, sacrifice and pain. In the ego's movie, the Universe is a somewhat hostile place where you are a victim of forces outside yourself over which you have little or no control.

Over the centuries, continued group belief in the ego's movie has created a somewhat insane reality in which we learn early that we have to be defensive, that we are not safe being fully alive and that we can't trust ourselves, other people or God. We have taken the internal splits and distortions we experience and projected them out into

102

the screen of external reality. It looks to most people that the best we can hope for is to somehow learn to cope or adjust to this "normal" level of insanity.

Healing this deep internal split and its mass projection onto "external reality" involves making changes on many levels, and in my experience, meditation can be of enormous benefit in this process.

Meditation is a very receptive or yin activity. Whether it be chanting a mantra such as OM Namah Shivia out loud, or repeating a mantra gently inside to one's self, one of the major purposes of all meditation is to allow us to transcend our mind and ego filter, open up awareness of our feminine side or connection with the Source and experience our "self" on the level of "Being," at the Source of all thoughts.

In Yogic philosophy this state of Being is considered to be at the source of all knowledge. It is called 'The Home of the Vedas' because it was through the awareness of this state that the Vedas were channeled. It is the home, or basis of all knowlege and creativity, the point at which all individuality merges in the oneness of infinite intelligence and being or God.

According to George Leonard in *The Silent Pulse*, we are constantly vibrating or pulsating in and out of this "other reality" thousands of times per second but we are unaware of it on the conscious level. By going inside and transcending the ego during meditation, we become consciously aware of this 'other side' of reality. If we can learn to be open and receptive, we do eventually become more conscious of our essence, or our connection to the Source and can create an opportunity for tremendous internal healing, not to mention stress release and relaxation.

In terms of our history as a species we have reached many levels of achievement, but a deep integrated sense of wholeness is still lacking for most people. In the East they have achieved a level of mastery of the inward stroke of meditation, but it does not seem to be backed up on the physical plane with action.

In the West we have achieved a high level of action and achievement on the physical plane, but it is rarely intuitively guided. It does not always come from an awareness of unity, or awareness of the whole. Believing our egos are real, and lacking an experience of connection to the Source, most of our action is based on fear, guilt, survival, defense, justification, the desire to be 'right,' the desire to please people or get approval, the desire for revenge, status, money, sex, control, and so on.

However, we are at a place in history now where we have the technology available to take the next step, to bridge the gap between intuition and action, and to create a holy relationship with ourselves that when reflected outward could become the beginning of the next stage of our evolutionary journey toward wholeness and unity.

There are many tools that we can use to support this transition and in a way, that is what this book is about. Sometimes the idea of loving God seems abstract and hard to fathom. However, one of the benefits of meditation, chanting and rebirthing is that they are all yin techniques that open our receptive side and allow us to experience our connection to God/the Source in a much more real and experiential way. Opening to our Being and our intuition and then trusting it and backing it up with action is a very powerful way of loving God. It may also be extremely essential not only to our transition into the next stage of evolution, but to our very survival as a species as well.

Loving God Through a Holy Relationship
by Yve Betar

As we all know, love is the greatest healer. Whenever we love, we experience an opportunity to grow, to expand our level of aliveness and to become more whole. Every relationship offers us a unique and powerful opportunity to heal ourselves if we are willing to take advantage of it. Those of you who have taken the LRT know that this is what the Training is all about. The "problem" has been that when we experience love, all our fears and patterns from the past can get activated. Th result is that we want love and intimacy and at the same time we fear it and unconsciously defend ourselves against it.

The *Course* says *"all healing is release from fear."* As we look within, we find that we all have the same bottom line fear. Underneath all our surface fears is the fear that we are separate—separate from God, from Spirit, from our own internal Source of love and aliveness. And

104

because we fear that we are separate from our own essence, we also fear that we are separate from each other. The *Course* calls this illusion of separation the *"detour into fear;"* and says that it was our original "mistake." The healing of this illusion it calls the *"atonement"* (at-one-ment) which means the undoing of all wrong thinking and the return to unified consciousness or wholeness. It says that to accomplish this the Universe immediately created the "Holy Spirit" (the spirit of energy of wholeness or healing). This is similar to the aspect of God the Hindus call "Shiva," the "destroyer of ignorance." Part of the process of becoming enlightened is to let go of our fear of being healed and invite this powerful energy into our lives and relationships.

THE ONLY REAL RELATIONSHIP In a way, we could say that there is only one real relationship going on for any of us. It is the relationship inside of us: the relationship between Spirit and the body that Spirit is bringing fully to life. All the other relationships we experience "externally" are a reflection of the one we experience "internally." Body and Spirit long to consummate their relationship, they long to unify, to become one. This is the immortality process, the process of raising the vibration of the body and aligning it with the vibration of Spirit. It is the process of letting go of all ego illusions and becoming fully whole, alive and in love. Spirit knows that the perfect completion of this process is inevitable. It is a patient, wise, loving and determined teacher, moving as deftly and quickly as we are willing to allow it to move.

The problem in this internal relationship is that as a result of the mistake of thinking separation is real, we have created a sense of false identity we call the "ego" based on a whole series of misperceptions, false conclusions, erroneous beliefs and defenses.

In order to complete the process of becoming whole and fulfill our purpose of becoming fully alive, body and spirit must move together through the illusion of the ego, see that it is not real, and allow it to disappear.

In order to accomplish this, we have to see that our ego beliefs in separation, limitation, lack, loss, guilt, pain, struggle, defense, and death are not real. We also have to realize that the level of passion, fulfillment and unity that we long for cannot be found "out there" where the ego is looking for it. It can't be found in our relationship with our egos or by trying to satisfy our ego desires. It can't be found in another person who we think will fulfill our lacks or needs, it can't be found in money, it can't be found in possessions, it can't be found in drugs, it can't be found in fame, it can't be found in glory, it can't be found in food, it can't be found in beautiful clothes. It can only be found inside. It's not that any of these things are necessarily wrong or bad—they are simply not the Source—and what we long for is the experience of our complete connection to the Source.

We have identified so strongly and so long with our ego beliefs that we feel split inside and seem to have two internal relationships. Our belief in separation leaves us feeling split off from Spirit, and the illusion of relationship with the ego may seem more real or more important to us than our relationship with who we really are.

SPECIAL AND HOLY RELATIONSHIPS Just as there seem to be two kinds of relationships we can experience inside, one real and one an illusion, there are two kinds we can experience outside. The *Course* calls these *"special"* and *"holy."* (The word "holy" comes from the same root as the words 'healed' and 'whole.') In the LRT we apply this to what we call "mortal" and "immortal" relationships. What's going on outside always reflects what's going on inside. This holds for relationships as well as anything else.

Special relationships are a reflection of our relationship with our egos—in fact, they are relationships between egos. Holy relationships are a reflection of our relationship with spirit—they are relationships between essences in the process of dissolving the illusion of separation.

The key difference between them lies in their purpose. The purpose of a holy or immortal relationship is healing, wholeness and unity. It is a relationship in which both partners are committed to seeing themselves and the other become all they can be. In a holy, immortal relationship partners do not see themselves as having separate interests, nor could they imagine that if one of them loses, the other could possibly win. The purpose of the relationship is to support both of them in becoming the immortal masters they are potentially capable of becoming, and in supporting each other in going through their process without 'buying into' their egos and making themselves or their process wrong. A holy relationship is a path to enlightenment.

"*. . . .an unholy relationship is based on differences, where each one thinks the other has what he has not. They come together, each to complete himself and rob the other. They stay until they think there is nothing left to steal, and then move on . . . A holy relationship starts from a different premise. Each one has looked within and seen no lack. Accepting his completion, he would extend it by joining with another, whole as himself.*" (Text, p. 435)

Sometimes it seems like people are afraid that a holy relationship is one that is pious, serious, celibate or boring; but fortunately, it is nothing of the kind. The *Course* says that "*God's will for us is perfect happiness*" and that we should not believe that "*happiness could ever be found in taking a road that leads away from it.*" A holy relationship is a road to happiness—that's its purpose. It is a relationship which supports us in letting go of ego illusions and experiencing more of our essence, of who we really are. It is a relationship in which we are committed to enlightenment and to the actualization of each person's highest potential. It is devoted to the purpose of having fun becoming all we can be, creating heaven on earth, and experiencing everyone's divinity and innocence (although it may bring up everything unlike these results along the way). Once we start realizing this kind of relationship is possible, how could we settle for anything else?

A special relationship, on the other hand, is subconciously designed to reinforce the illusion of separation. It tends to be based on the dynamics of need-obligate, sacrifice and manipulation through guilt. Within it partners feel they cannot share themselves completely and tend to withhold from each other, afraid to tell each other the complete truth. It ultimately seems to diminish its participants. It leaves them feeling less alive and passionate and more guilty and afraid. They end up rationalizing their feelings of separation, settling for less than they really want, and getting to be "right" about how unsatisfying life or relationships can be.

HOW DO YOU GO ABOUT CREATING A HOLY RELATIONSHIP?
In this world (the ego-based reality in which most of us live) most relationships start out as special relationships. They are transformed

as we begin to understand that our reality is a reflection of our thoughts, our beliefs, and our own sense of identity. Transforming our relationships is a big commitment and involves being willing to change our entire belief system, including our sense of who we are, as well as developing the ability to trust the Universe and expect miracles.

Illusions seem real only because we believe in them. Our beliefs hold them in our experiencce and keep them manifest on the physical plane. In order to make illusions disappear, we have to be willing to withdraw our belief in them, for it is only our belief that gives them life. We have to be willing to see differently, to see that they are not real and stop acting as if they are. It can seem like quite a challenge, but the results are worth it. It might even seem like an impossible task, but as the *Course* reminds us, we do not have to do it alone. Our job is to be willing to trust, commit and surrender to the process, and the Holy Spirit will do the rest. I experience this as true; and that once we make the commitment, (even though we may experience doubt along the way), we can count on miracles and an amazing level of support from the Universe to get us through to the other side.

RECIPE FOR A HOLY RELATIONSHIP

1. Commit your relationship to the single purpose of supporting each of you in becoming more whole, alive, happy, fulfilled and enlightened. Turn your relationship over to the Holy Spirit.

2. Work together on changing the ego beliefs that do not support your purpose and only create illusions of limitation, separation, guilt and fear.

3. Practice seeing your interests as the same, always going for the highest thought and creating win-win situations whenever the illusion of conflict appears in your relationship.

4. Consciously and lovingly support each other in letting go of behaviors that constrict your energy flow and reinforce the ego's illusion of separation. These include:
• withholding or lying
• blaming (each other or anyone else)

- thinking loss is real (every apparent loss is a gain not yet recognized)
- holding onto guilt
- manipulation through guilt
- holding on to the illusions of the past and using them as our reference point
- acting out of obligation (this eventually leads to resentment)
- saying yes when you mean no and no when you mean yes
- doing things you don't really want to do in order to get approval or avoid disapproval
- struggling
- defending and justifying
- judging
- making yourself wrong
- sacrificing
- being motivated by fear or guilt
- needing to be needed
- perceiving others as being lacking or needy
- saving and rescuing people (learn to be supportive without the invalidation of rescue)
- needing to be right or making being right more important than being happy

5. Become fast friends.

6. Make your relationship a top priority in your life. Have fun together. If you both have busy schedules, schedule in time for pleasure together, time to share and be intimate, time to be outrageous, time to relax.

7. Recognize that your partner and his/her reality is also part of your mind. See him/her as your perfect mirror and know that he/she is not separate from you.

8. Practice forgiveness and gratitude constantly. Remember that if you can forgive one person totally and completely and hold no grievances, you can forgive everyone. If you can love one person totally and completely, you can love everyone. When you can see only your brother's innocence as real, you will be able to see your own innocence as real. It's time to withdraw the power of our belief from the

illusion and enter the kingdom of Heaven on earth together, for it cannot be entered alone.

I want to close with some quotes from the *Course* that I read for the wedding of some wonderful friends of ours, Gayle and Pierre Charbonier, when they were committing to their holy immortal relationship. These quotes are taken from the text, Chapter 20, "The Vision of Holiness."

"In this world, God's Son comes closest to himself in a holy relationship. There he finds the certainty his father has in him . . .

"The ark of peace is entered two by two, yet the beginning of another world goes with them. Each holy relationship must enter here, to learn its special function in the Holy Spirit's Plan, now that it shares his purpose. And as this purpose is fulfilled, a new world arises in which sin can enter not, and where the Son of God can enter without fear . . .

"Here there is only holiness and joining without limit. For what is heaven but union, direct and perfect, and without the veil of fear upon it? Here we are one, looking with perfect gentleness upon each other and on ourselves. Here all thoughts of separation between us become impossible. You who were prisoners in separation are now made free in Paradise. And here I would unite with you, my friend, my brother and my Self.

"Each of you now will lead the other to the Father as surely as God created his Son holy, and kept him so. In your brother is the promise of your immortality. See him as sinless, and there can be no fear in you.

"So do the parts of God's Son gradually join in time, and with each joining is the end of time brought nearer. Each miracle of joining is a mighty herald of eternity. No one who has a single purpose, unified and sure, can be afraid.

"Each herald of eternity sings of the end of sin and fear . . . Two voices raised together call to the hearts of everyone, to let them beat as one. And in that single heartbeat is the unity of love proclaimed and given welcome. Peace to your holy relationship, which has the power to hold the unity of the Son of God together. You give to one another for everyone, and in your gift is everyone made glad.

"The Holy Spirit's temple is not a body, but a relationship."

God and Children

by Gene & Helen Aptekar

Founders of KLS (Kids' Love Shop)
A Version of the LRT for Children

When Sondra first asked us to write a chapter on "God and Children" for her new book, we didn't believe that she actually wanted US to write something for her. "Why US? We're not writers. What do WE know?" was our first reaction. We laughed, we expressed how much we really love Sondra, and we forgot about it. But Sondra had planted a seed.

A few weeks later, while we were flying down to Florida to do a KLS, we had this great thought: Add a section on GOD to tomorrow's training and have the assistants write down what the kids say, and we'll get material for Sondra's chapter directly from the kids. It was inspiring! We tried it out first in Florida and have done it in every training since then, in Atlanta, Denver, and New York. The results have always been the same; the kids love doing it, the room feels real warm, loving, and peaceful, and the sharing is great.

Even though their bodies are small, they do think about "grown up" things. Here are the main thoughts kids have about GOD. The responses were culled from 165 kids, ages 8 to 15.

The main thought I have about GOD is:
1. God always forgives.
2. God is beautiful both inside and outside.
3. God's presence is everywhere.
4. God is always there to talk to.
5. God is very caring.
6. God loves everyone unconditionally.
7. God could be young or old. He is ageless.
8. God is love.
9. God is our inner peace.
10. God is the light within us.
11. God only does good.
12. God wants us to use His power.

13. God is wonderful for creating feathers.
14. God doesn't always make it come out the way we
    expect it to.

When the kids were given the opportunity to tell God something, some asked questions, some expressed gratitude, and some acknowledged God. And some said . . . "The thing I'd like to tell God is, 'I forgive you for making my cat run away.' "

Questions: Why is there war? Why is there killing? Why is there crime? Why did You create us?

Gratitudes: Thank you for my life. Thank you for giving us freedom of choice. Thank you for watching over me, my family, and my friends. Thank you for all the living things.

Acknowledgments: I think you did a great job with the universe, especially the earth. I just want to tell Him that I love Him.

One of the areas we adults can learn a lot about from the kids is in letting more God into our lives. There is no doubt in our minds that kids are closer to the God inside of them. Yes, you can see some doubts, some judgments, some hatred, some ego, but for the most part their innocence just keeps on shining. ". . . .And a little child shall lead the way."

Our children are leading the way. They are eager to share their favorite way of letting more God into their life. Since they are closer to God they really know . . . Who wants to follow?

"My favorite way to let more God into my life is:
1. be more loving.
2. trust God more.
3. acknowledge God more.
4. talk to God more.
5. express gratitudes more.
6. get rebirthed.

112

7. be less judgmental.
8. enjoy my life more.
9. enjoy other people more.
10. laugh more.
11. play more.
12. be myself more.
13. by forgiving every thorn bush that ever pricked me.
14. by being nice to nature.
15. by giving up blame.
16. by practicing forgiveness.
17. by meditating more.
18. by sharing myself more with other people.

Surely out of these 18 suggestions every grown-up could find one thing that they could do. And wouldn't it be nice if we acknowledge our children for their leadership in this area!

Thank you, Sondra; we consider it a blessing that we get to do a section on God in the KLS (Kids' Love Shop) which is already filled with so many blessings. You are a constant inspiration. We love you forever.

CHAPTER 9

THE MASTER AS A PATH TO PURE JOY

Some people mistakenly think that if you have a guru or master, then you have to give your power away . . . . In my experience, nothing could be farther from the truth. My experience is that the master helps us to achieve our own power and stand on our own feet; and this happens as fast as you can take it. In the presence of the master we are able to touch our own wholeness and our own perfection faster. As you get closer to the master, you find less and less of him and more of yourself. The guru is a mirror. Only in this case, it might feel like you see yourself magnified times one thousand or more. It can be very intense. You have to face yourself like never before.

For me it was a deep deep yearning for the truth, a deep longing to know perfect love, a desire to know all that life could be, a craving for divinity and pure joy that caused me to be a seeker. My experience was that Babaji, who responded to this yearning and longing in my heart, helped dispel my ignorance, my limitations, my fears, my karma, my ego, and all that kept me from knowing my own inner divine nature. I could not resist his outpouring of Divine Love. Why should I, when it was there for the asking? I asked and I was answered. He was and is a gift to me and he is a gift to all humanity. He has awakened me. He has helped me to become strong so I can stand on my own two feet.

The true Guru is merely a path to your own inner self.

THIS IS BABAJI!

CHAPTER 10
WHO IS BABAJI?

All of my books are dedicated to Babaji, who is my teacher, guide, inspiration, and best example of Pure Joy. Babaji, also named Sri Sri 1008 Bhagwan Herakhan Wale Baba, is an immortal maha avatar and yogi master ("avatar" means "descent of the Divine into matter"). Babaji is an emanation of Divine light, who, out of compassion, manifested in human form on earth to urge humanity to progress on the path of truth, simplicity, love, and service to mankind. He is the power of the Eternal Father, Mother, and Divine Child. He can assume any form He wishes and can change that form at any time. He is known as the historical Sada Shiva in Hindu religious literature. In fulfillment of ancient scriptural and prophetic predictions, He materialized a youthful body in 1970 in a cave near the village of Hairakhan in the Kumaon foothills of the Himalayas. There are Indian devotees who tell stories of this, and Yogananda wrote about him in the book *Autobiography of a Yogi*.

Babaji was accessible for 14 years on this last visit. And yet He has not left, because He does not come and go. He was, and is, omnipresent. His form is limitless and beyond the scope of time. He is the essence of all religions and transcends every belief. He teaches through vibrations and direct experience in a way that words can not express. To try to explain Him on paper seems inadequate. To be with Him or experience Him answers all questions. It is my desire to share Him; and since I have had so many requests, I will attempt to do so here by also including words from those who lived near Him for years and years.

It is my humblest desire to make it known to you that any story I relate to you about Babaji is given with the intention to let you know that He is just as available for you and for all as He is for me. His healing presence is omnipresent in the whole universe, and you may have miracles in your life with it the way I have in mine (although each person's relationship with that aspect of his higher self is, however, unique to him).

I wish to include you in my relationship with Babaji as an inspiration, as a way of spreading more joy, and especially to remind you that this is available always to everyone.

This next section was written by Ram Dass Giri, a yogi who spent five years at Sri Babaji's ashram in Herakhan. I am pleased to introduce you to Babaji in this chapter, and now let's read what Ram Dass Giri has to say as he introduces you to Babaji:

Om Haidiyakhandi
by Ram Dass Giri

Pure joy is our natural condition. Some of our brothers and sisters have said that pure joy is our *birthright* and this is relatively correct. Yet, seen in its largest perspective, pure joy is that which *gives* birth to us.

We are a spontaneous expression of the most evolved, most mysterious creative force of life itself. None of the saints and sages who have visited the earth plane have ever been able to use words to express *why* this happens. The most frequent communication of why this happens emanates from them as laughter, gleefulness, tears of joy, a twinkling eye and the most profound transmission of cosmic silence.

To sit in utter stillness at the feet of the Master with a quiet mind and an adoring heart are prerequisites for the dissolution of all afflicting emotions that create noise patterns which obscure the extremely subtle yet all pervasive state of pure joy.

The Master may appear as a body. It may appear as a light or a sound or a feeling, yet, regardless of the form It may take, it is located in the depth of the heart. The Divine Master is pure joy Itself, congealed into a form that is recognizable. The more one focuses on it, the more concrete it becomes.

Prana (life force) has its home base in the body at the level of the heart. The masters of China have stated that the energy which congeals in the body to form the heart is pure joy itself. In India, the heart is seen not only as pure joy but also the seat or home of the Divine Spark that has pulsed into existence as a "separate" form. It is called jivatma—the Soul in singularity. It is from this Spark of pure joy that the rest of our bodily being arises.

If you lie down and close your eyes, placing your hands on your heart or on a blood vessel, the pulsing in the heart becomes apparent. Now, consider, are you responsible for that beating heart? How did it begin? What started that pulse? Does it have a beginning and an end—a limited existence? With continued investigation you will find that prior to the formation of body tissue there is a pulsing, the pulsing of creation—the Creatrix of the Universe—the Divine Mother. And if you continue to investigate that pulsing you may experience the moment of "arising" that gives birth to the creative power of life Itself. It is a never ending process of waking from stillness and dissolving into that stillness again—the stillness of pure joy.

Within that stillness there exists an unimaginably vast potential for knowingness—a knowingness that has no sense of separation from ultimate joy—yet, may congeal itself into a recognizable mass of consciousness. This is the state of "Sada Shiv," as the Sanskrit scholars would say. In English we would say the "I am that" consciousness. And eventually, that consciousness can, at its own will, congeal a physical body into existence amidst the phenomenal world. That physical body is known as Haidakhan Baba, the Mahavatar.

All humankind experiences the progression of consciousness into human form, yet Mahavatar Babaji is one of the very, very few who manifests a body directly from the state of pure joy.

He is the Mahavatar, the "greatest manifestation of Divine Joy into human form." He is pure joy Itself. He has been with us since the dawn of creation.

On certain occasions He will manifest a human form when human beings become too insensitive to know and feel His presence as their original condition. At all other times, He remains in the Unmanifest state, yet is experienced in the delight of a child with a puppy, the warmth of a lover's embrace, the bliss of meditation—the opening of the heart in any form. He is the essence of all that you are . . . pure . . . purer . . . purest joy.

Babaji is Pure Joy

There is a ceremonial prayer called the Aarti which is sung in Sanskrit. One of the lines that I love the most from it is this: "Thou art a never failing spring of bliss."

That is, and always has been, my experience of Babaji, who has been with us on earth in human form countless times since life began. Some of his lifetimes are well-known—Shiva, Ram, and Krishna, for example. In other lifetimes, he was known to relatively few. Jesus is said to have visited Babaji in Benares during Jesus' travels and studies in the East. It was there that Babaji shaved Jesus' head and blessed Him before Jesus started His ministry.

In many sacred texts it was written that, when righteousness declines, God creates for Himself a body and comes to live on Earth. He appears and makes Himself known to those who seek Him. The Bhagavad-Gita 4:9 reads as follows:

> *When righteousness is weak and faints and uprighteousness exults in pride, then my Spirit arises on earth.*
>
> *For the salvation of those who are good, for the destruction of evil in men, for the fulfillment of the kingdom of righteousness, I come to this world in the ages that pass.*
>
> *He who knows my birth as God and who knows my sacrifice when he leaves his mortal body, goes no more from death to death, for he, in truth, comes to me.*

The Gospel of St. Thomas says:

> *If you see him who has not been born of a woman, throw your face to the ground and worship him—he is your father.*

In fulfillment of ancient scriptural and prophetic predictions, Babaji reappeared in a youthful body in 1970 in a cave near the village of Haidahkan in the Kumaon foothills of the Himalayas, and he stayed in Haidakhan until 1984. Haidakhan is the ancestral home of Lord Shiva. In 1922 he ended one lifetime by disappearing into the convergence of the Gauri and Kali Rivers on the Napalese border before a group of followers. In 1970, when he reappeared, he climbed to the top of Mount Kailash and sat for 45 days without sleeping or eating. Then he began to teach his message to villagers who gathered around him.

During the 1970s and '80s, he oversaw the construction of the Ashram and Gardens. When he left again on Valentine's Day 1984, he asked one of the devotees to watch over some of the items in Haidakhan for him until his eventual return.

Babaji can assume any form he wishes and can change that form at any time. He is the embodiment of the power of both the Eternal Father and Mother, and on one occasion *after* he "left" in 1984, he appeared to me—as a *woman* walking on air. This was the most incredibly beautiful female I have ever seen in all lifetimes—that was my response—and yet it was definitely the same energy of Babaji which I have always felt with him.

Since he is an Immortal Spirit Avatar, who has the ability to dematerialize and rematerialize at will, he can obviously turn his body into a ball of light and travel anywhere in the universe. He can also bi-locate and be in two places at once. His physical bodies change rapidly, partly because he processes his devotees' karmas rapidly. He can also drop a body whenever he feels like it for whatever purpose. He always has a sense of humor, and on February 14, on *Valentine's Day,* he said, "I am going to explode my heart and give a piece to everyone"—and consciously gave the "appearance" of a kind of heart attack. This, I believe, he did to process out the death urge of devotees and to force us to become independent. I was not upset at all because I knew that it was a "Lila"—a divine play of God in human form—and that he knew exactly what he was doing. Probably he was merging his electrons with the universe, fortunately, for us.

For the following two weeks, he began appearing to me in different bodies, sometimes when I was asleep, but even when I was awake, to remind me that he was not really dead—which I knew anyway. Since then he has appeared to many of my students in Rebirthings and at night.

For the present, life goes on as usual at his ashram in Haidakhan and at all his other ashrams and centers all over the world. The Western World was first introduced to Babaji in 1946 with the publication of Paramahansa Yogananda's fascinating accounting *The Autobiography of a Yogi* (especially chapters 33 and 34). You can also read *Hariakhan Baba: Known and Unknown*, by Baba Hari Dass, published by the Sri Rama Foundation in Davis, California.

As soon as we are mentally connected with a Supreme Power like Babaji or Jesus, our mind is absorbed in God, and we are filled with Divine Glory. Imagine how absolutely great it feels to be filled with Divine Glory. Listen to the song entitled "Babaji" sung by the rock group Supertramp on the album *In the Quietest Moments."*

Babaji is beyond all religion. He is the Essence of all religions, the Source of Religions. He teaches that all faiths ultimately lead to the same goal. Babaji transcends every belief. He teaches through vibrations and direct experience in a way that words cannot express. The only religion you could possibly call it is the Eternal Religion of Humanity. He came to show, by his example, how to live.

His teachings reflect man's spontaneous urge to acknowledge the unity with the Supreme Spirit. Spiritual practices for achieving this unity are basic natural practices like work and service to God and humanity, repetition of God's Holy Names (chanting mantras), devotion to God in constant awareness of the Supreme Spirit through remembrance of God, and living in love, truth, and simplicity.

He taught that through the practice of Karma Yoga (work dedicated to God), man purifies and protects himself. "Work is Worship" is a statement he often made. He taught a philosophy of *action*. He would often say, "An idle man is like a dead man."

He always said that the simplest and most powerful method for bringing peace and understanding to the mind is through the singing or saying of the mantra *Om Namaha Shivai*. To quote Babaji about this mantra:

This is the Mahamantra, the great original mantra, given by the Lord to humanity. Everyone should repeat it. It can be

■   a lotus flower

■   a Dhanush, or bow;

■   a Chakra, or wheel;

■   the crescent moon (indicating perfect mind control);

■   all the signs of the Zodiac;

■   the serpent (representing wisdom and eternity, as well as fearlessness and immortality);

■   the sun;

■   an octagon;

■   a hatchet;

■   an eagle;

■   a club;

■   the planetary system, with sun and moon at its center.

These marks fulfill the predictions delivered long ago that when Shiva was next to appear in human form, he would have these symbols and a scar on his lower right leg and upper left arm (which he did).

His spiritual significance has always been beyond comprehension. "Shiva" means eternally happy and auspicious, the God without second who has been moving in this world in his form since creation, watchful for eternity over the welfare of mankind and the universe. He is described as ever-pure, changeless, all-pervading, eternal, the immortal essence of the universe, the universal Self, the self resplendent light of Lights, the embodiment of wisdom, capable of doing anything at any moment, or whatever magnitude.

Yogananda wrote of Babaji materializing a palace in the Himalayas out of his thought waves. You can visit this location where we celebrate the Divine Mother Festival every year. The temple is built in the same shape as the one that Babaji materialized on the same spot! It is surrounded by the beautiful Himalayas. Babaji said if you visit this spot during the Divine Mother Festival, it is so powerful that one day equals 12 years of clearing your karma!

To see Babaji is the highest honor of a lifetime. To visit any of his ashrams is also a great gift. Once you do, your life will never, ever be the same. However, the value of your visit will be determined by your own personal purification. Being in the energy of the guru is just getting yourself magnified by thousands. So if you go with doubt, you get more doubt. If you go with an open heart, you get everything. It is a rapid spiritual progress that is in store for you if you surrender.

You do not give your power away to the guru—that is not the purpose. The guru teaches you to become your own guru as fast as you can take it. The guru teaches you who *you* are—which is why Babaji said, "I am nobody's guru and yet I am the guru of gurus." The guru helps clear your karma. The guru helps you keep your ego in check. The guru helps you get off the birth-death cycle. The guru helps teach you spiritual mastery. The guru helps you get out of misery. The guru helps you to protect yourself. The guru helps you learn to clear your body and maintain health. The guru enhances your creativity. The guru is Joy—*Pure Joy.*

Why not think about going to Haidakhan, Babaji's home? Babaji said,

> *This is the holiest religious place in the world, holier even than Benares. The water of this river purifies you from all sins. Haidakhan is the birthplace of all yogis and the deity of Yogis as the source of inspiration. By merely sitting here you reap the results of hundreds of lifetimes of penance. Those who live here for some time automatically get many kinds of yogic powers. Those who have darshan at this place will have all their wishes fulfilled—both material and spiritual desires. They will have the assurance of complete success.*
>
> *But only he can come here in whose life a turning point has come, when the spiritual energy is rising. Lord Rama said only he can come here who has done great penance in his previous lives . . .*

If you want to make the annual trip with me, please contact RAM-LOTI, P.O. Box 95, Crestone, CO 81131 or phone (719) 256-4108 at the U.S. Ashram. You must be an LRT graduate and have been adequately rebirthed as preparation. The address of the ashram is as follows: Haidakhan Vishwa Mahadham, Via Kathgodam Dist. Nainital., U.P. 263126, India.

A Little Speech from Babaji

We are all made up of the five elements.
We are all from one spirit.
The birthright of the whole human race
Is to love and follow God.
In every way we are one humanity.
One human family.
Being a human being is the most
Important element in life.
It is the only valid religion:
Be an example of tolerance and forgiveness.
                                        —Sri Babaji

A Speech by Babaji

Love and serve all humanity.
Assist everyone.
Be cheerful. Be courteous.
Be a dynamo of irrepressible happiness.
See God and good in every face.
There is no Saint without a past.
There is no sinner without a future.
Praise every soul.
If you cannot praise someone . . .
Let them pass out of your life.
Be original. Be inventive.
Dare, dare, and then dare more.
Do not imitate. Stand on your own ground.
Do not lean on the borrowed staff of others.
Think your own thoughts.
Be yourself.
All perfection and all virtues of the
Diety are hidden inside you.
Reveal them.
The Saviour, also, is already within you.
Reveal Him.
Let His grace emancipate you.
Let your life be that of a rose.
Though silent it speaks in the language of
fragrance.
                                        —Baba

THIS IS MUNIRAJ!

CHAPTER 11
WHO IS SRI MUNIRAJ?

Trilok Singh, Sri Babaji's closest devotee, was given the title *MUNIRAJ* by Sri Babaji. It means "King of Sages." Babaji said that Sri Muniraj is no longer bound by the law of birth and rebirth. By his own will he came to earth to help humanity. Babaji charged him with the task of continuing his work, and mentioned further that Muniraj is an incarnation of Dattatreya, the first master who was a combination of Vishnu, Shiva, and Rama.

In recent times there was another guru who entered Muniraj's body. His name was guru Om Karnath Sita Ram Dass, who had 62 ashrams in India and thousands and thousands of devotees. He accepted Babaji before he took Samadhi, and Babaji gave him permission to enter Muniraj's body. We asked Muniraj how it felt when that happened, and he then asked us, "How does it feel to add water to water?"

Muniraj was born in the area of Chilyanaula, where the Divine Mother Festival is held. Muniraj was given birth there on purpose because it is called the Land of the Gods. It is a very ancient space going back before the time of Rama. It was the Divine Mother's home 20,000 years ago. On the spot where the temple is Babaji gave initiation to Lahiri Mahasaya (Yogananda's guru's guru) and near where Babaji materialized the palace out of his thought waves. Muniraj gave the land back to Babaji and the devotees.

Muniraj has been called by some the "King of Silence," for he says little. However, to be with him is to understand why he was chosen. On my first trek to find Babaji, I met Muniraj in the town of Haldwani in the province of Uttar Pradesh at the foothills of the Himalayas. Muniraj "checked me over" and put me on the right path. I remember that my first thought about him was, "This is the most peaceful man I have ever met on earth!" Once, years later, Babaji made me wait under a tree for Muniraj for approximately 12 hours. When I finally saw Muniraj hiking up the riverbed toward us at the ashram, I felt incredible joy. That was also the day I saw Babaji himself *Pranam* (lying face down at his feet) to Muniraj. Muniraj was the only one I ever saw Babaji bow to.

Sri Muniraj now represents and carries on Babaji's work. When asked about Babaji's next reappearance, Muniraj said, "Certainly he will reappear. In the meantime, we try to spread his message and live accordingly in order to be prepared for his reappearance."

THIS IS SHASTRIJI!

CHAPTER 12
WHO IS SHASTRIJI?

Shastriji is Babaji's "High Priest." He is the mouthpiece of Babaji. He is, along with Muniraj, the pure essence of Babaji. He is, according to Babaji, one of the most learned men on earth. He is a Saint and everything you imagine a Saint to be! Furthermore, he is an ayurvedic doctor, astrologer, and pure clairvoyant. He has great wisdom of the Vedas and their rites and is an interperter of Indian myths and the Santana Dharma, as the Indians call their religion. About the books he has written, he says that they are pure inspiration: all of them are in mantric verses. His main work of historical content is a vision about Shri Babaji's incarnations through all times. The book "Sadashiva Charitamrit" has over 1200 pages and is now being translated into English. Another work, the *Haidakhandesvar Sapta Sati*, 700 Verses in Praise of the Divine Mother of Haidakhan, is available in English and German. I am very honored that he has allowed me to publish a few of my favorite verses from that book for your joy and pleasure on page 00. Shastriji also fulfilled my request to write something just for this book. He wrote "How To Love God and Be Happy" on the following page. Later he agreed to let me publish his amazing speech at Schweibenalp, the ashram in Switzerland. These brilliant speeches help us to understand Babaji and the rituals and ceremonies he taught us.

Babaji once said that Shastriji has been a poet in all life times. He certainly does have exalted thoughts. To me, he is in a constant state

135

of prayer. He is constantly praying out loud. To be with him feels like living a miracle. Babaji said he is one of the purest men on Earth.

Spiritual Poetry in Praise of the Divine Mother

VERSES TO THE DIVINE MOTHER

Oh Devi, You are prosperity and the Power of Increase. To You we bow. You are radiant light; we bow to You. Benefactress of the world, We bow to You.

Salutation to You, Mother of the universes; we bow to You who lives in them forever . . . through all the ages. Your form is beyond the decay of time; inherent in everything, You are immortal. You are beyond being known, of unfathomable mystery. Great Mother, we bow to You.

The universe is full of Your glory, Oh Mother; to You we bow who is beautified with that glory. You are the Goddess of every desire, taking even the forms of desire, fulfilling them all. We bow to You.

As Sri Vasant, Goddess of spring, You give happiness to the world and all its beings. You know the root of all the troubles in the world and support the entire universe, being its central axis. You dwell on the island of Manipura. To You we bow.

It is You who churn the mind, You who are the giver of sexual desire and it is You who grant great fortune. Glory be to You, whose names are Medini, the earth, and Mahima Devi, Goddess of Majesty. We bow to You again and again as Mandavi, as Mahadevi, the great Goddess, and as Manjula, Goddess of Beauty.

You bestow Your grace on perfected beings and on Yoginis who, too, are aspects of You when they take care of Children. The universe bows to You who annihilates the pain of the world.

136

Oh, Mother, You are the luminosity of the moon and the sun's divine light is Yours; even the pure radiance of the planets is a reflection of You. You are the fire's ardour and the softness of water, the strength in the earth; Yours is the Power to sustain the earth. Yours is the Power in the universe and it is You who, in Lord Visnu, is the preserving Energy.

PRAISES TO THE DIVINE MOTHER

You are the one who takes the form of truth-consciousness-bliss. You are the purity of this world: to You we bow, Oh Devi. You are the embodiment of beauty. Oh, Goddess, You are Sinhika, mother of the titan Rahu, and are also known in the world as "She who speaks the truth."

You bestow happiness on all the universes and shower grace on Your devotees and give them nourishment in plenty. You are radiant with divine effulgence. As the fierce Candi, Goddess of destruction, You annihilate fear. To You the supreme Energy of Lord Narayana, we bow again and again.

As the supreme Being, oh timeless Goddess, Mother Haidakhandes-vari, You are the Mistress of all yoginis; we pray to You that all the goddesses would have compassion on us and grace us with their benevolence.

You always reside in the heart of all beings as their own self. As Maya, the cosmic illusion, You adorn life with the most beautiful glow; You are ever perfect in Your divinity as supreme knowledge; YOU ARE THE ULTIMATE POINT IN THE INFINITY OF COSMIC SPACE. As the universal Self, You shower the rain of divine nectar on the world and let the rain of bliss drown all the fears of this world. Oh Mother, we seek refuge in You.

Oh Mahalaksmi, Goddess of great magnificence, Your eyes have the beauty of the lotus; come and bless me with one glance of mercy and give me initiation. Oh Mother, You clear the path of obstacles of him who has obtained Your mercy. You are the fount of true knowledge and grant boons to him who is under Your protection. Oh, Savesvari, protect me.

VERSES FROM HAIDAKHANDI SPTA SATI: SEVENHUNDRED VERSES IN PRAISE OF THE DIVINE MOTHER OF HAIDAKHAN

OM, I BOW TO HER WHO GIVES JOY TO THE SOUL..
OM, I BOW TO HER WHOSE FORM IS BLISS..
OM, I BOW TO HER WHO IS FULL OF BOUNDLESS MERCY.
OM, I BOW TO HER WHO IS THE SUPREME MOTHER.
OM, I BOW TO HER WHO FULFILLS ALL DESIRES.
OM, I BOW TO HER WHO BESTOWS GOOD FORTUNE.
OM, I BOW TO HER WHO IS THE EMBODIMENT
  OF KNOWLEDGE.
OM, I BOW TO HER WHO IS PROSPERITY.
OM, I BOW TO THE GODDESS OF HEAVEN.
OM, I BOW TO THE DIVINE ENERGY.
OM, I BOW TO HER WHO REMOVES ALL FEAR.
OM, I BOW TO HER WHO GIVES DIVINE PERFECTION.
OM, I BOW TO THE ETERNAL ONE.
OM, I BOW TO HER WHO GIVES LIBERATION.
OM, I BOW TO THE GODDESS WHO PROTECTS.
OM, I BOW TO THE GODDESS OF FORTUNE.
OM, I BOW TO HER WHO IS THE EMBODIMENT
  OF MAGNIFICENCE.
OM, I BOW TO HER WHO GIVES WEALTH TO ALL.
OM, I BOW TO HER WHO REMOVES THE TROUBLES
  OF THE UNIVERSE.
OM, I BOW TO HER WHO IS ROYAL MAJESTY.
OM, I BOW TO HER WHO IS SAVIOR OF ALL.
OM, I BOW TO HER WHO ALWAYS SHOWERS NECTAR
  OF GRACE.
OM, I BOW TO HER WHO IS THE EXPERIENCER OF JOY.
OM, I BOW TO HER WHO ELIMINATES ALL SICKNESS.

OM, I BOW TO HER WHO RESIDES IN THE CAVE
  OF HAIDAKHAN.
OM, I BOW TO HER WHO IS ETERNAL.
OM, I BOW TO HER WHO IS IMMORTAL.
OM, I BOW TO HER WHO IS EVER VICTORIOUS.
OM, I BOW TO HER WHO IS THE SOURCE
  OF SUPREME LIGHT.
OM, I BOW TO HER WHO IS THE EMBODIMENT OF GLORY.
OM, I BOW TO HER WHO IS THE EMBODIMENT OF ART.
OM, I BOW TO HER WHO IS THE EMBODIMENT
  OF FORGIVENESS.
OM, I BOW TO HER WHO IS THE EMBODIMENT OF PEACE.
OM, I BOW TO HER WHO RESIDES IN THE SPINAL CORD.
OM, I BOW TO HER WHO IS THE EMBODIMENT OF JOY,
  THE OCEAN OF JOY.
OM, I BOW TO HER WHO GIVES ABUNDANTLY THE NECTAR
  OF JOY!

Shastriji Speaks on Loving God

HOW TO LOVE GOD AND BE HAPPY The Divine is the Absolute
element of the soul and the soul loves the soul utmost. In the Vedas
it is mentioned that "a husband is a beloved not because he is a husband, but he fulfills the desire and hence he is a beloved; a wife is
beloved not because she is a wife, but as she is the vessel to fulfill
the desires so she is a beloved." With this Vedic Mantra the sage Rishi
Yajnavalka gave the teachings of the Soul element to his wife Aatreyei.
He also made it clear that in this life the Soul is the most beloved
and what the Soul loves, one loves all the time. This Soul is a small
atom of the Source—The Great Soul. That's why when a human being
loves the parents, husband, wife, son, or daughter, he or she is con-
templating a form of the Lord in his beloved relationships, and finds
happiness. A man loves no one more than his own kith and kin. All
relationships, love and the things of joy are nothing in comparison
to the Divine Love. It is beyond everything! That's why to contem-
plate or meditate on the Divine all the time is the highest form of

139

discipline. In every little thing, when a man sees the Presence of the Divine, he will surely be able to love them all. In every form, when he loves the Divine, then only can he find true joy and happiness. For example, when a chick has just hatched from the egg, or a new-born calf awaits its mother's return to feed it, they are looking one-pointedly in the direction of the mother's arrival; also like a newly wedded wife whose husband has gone off to battle, she waits for him to return and during this period of separation she endures much agony and turmoil. So it is that the same thing happens when a man's soul starts to long to be one with the Divine and become One within, for then only can he truly become joyous and know bliss and he has made the union total. The feeling of separation disappears completely! This is truly the ultimate bliss and it is the great "Ananda" (Joy). In truth, total surrender from the heart is the element of great joy!

—Shastriji

12 June, 1986

A TRANSCRIPTION OF SRI SHASTRIJI'S SPEECHES AT SIDD-HASHRAM SCHWEIBENALP, SWITZERLAND, MAY, 1985

This beautiful spot, Schweibenalp, is located in the Bernese Alps. This consecrated sacred place is an ashram of Sri Babaji, offering all of the basic devotional practices and traditional rituals and festivals. Schweibenalp also maintains its character as a Center of Unity. Every religious form or spiritual practice is respected and openly welcomed in addition to Babaji's Hindu practices.

Schweibenalp is devoted to transforming personal, social and spiritual consciousness. Schweibenalp has as one goal to realize a har-monious balance between family life, community interaction and reli-gious discipline. One of the unique aspects of Schweibenalp is combination of ashram routine with a wide palette of seminars, spiritual healing and purification techniques. One can have a won-derful transforming experience at this power spot.

Shastriji Speaks:
Ladies and Gentlemen!

Today, when on this most auspicious occasion, on this most sacred earth, I set my foot, I felt the vibrations of this ashram and all of you, I can't tell you how happy I was!

With the grace of Sri Mahaprabhuji's lotus feet I have visited many sacred ashrams and had the occasion to be on sacred sites many times. But when I set my foot on this most sacred place, I entered such a consciousness that I forgot myself, the universe, I forgot the world and just felt bliss and happiness so deeply that I cannot put it into words. At the same time the thought started coming into my mind and heart: "Who is this great man who has done tapas (penance) for thousands of years? With whose great tapasya with the inspiration of the Divine Mother Jagadishvari Shri Siddha Siddheshwari and of Lord Haidakhan has arrived here and made this Her sacred place? And believe me when I say that this place will one day become the most leading centre of the Western world. And as far as knowledge is concerned, the whole world believes India is the leading country. And for the material knowledge, the Western world is foremost. But I feel that knowledge, the sun of knowledge, will rise from this place in the world.

The incarnation of Lord Herakhandi Bihari Deva has taken place to give the benefit of true knowledge and bliss to the whole world. With His infinite compassion and grace Sri Mahaprabhuji remained with us for more than 5,700 days. It was His divine grace that He gave darshan to thousands of people, but at the same time there were many who were there but did not have the grace to have His darshan and when He wanted to grace some people, He called them from thousands of miles to Him. Some were called from thousands and thousands of miles away, some were just a few hundred miles away, some were a few miles away, and some were just near but they just did not have the occasion to have His darshan, because it was just not their destiny.

141

Sri Mahaprabhuji, when He was with us in His physical body, gave to us the ultimate root of the Vedic principles which prevailed during the Treta Yuga and Dvapara Yuga, that is about 5,000 and 2,000 years ago, in a very simple manner: He made them available to the world, to the common man. He was the Supreme Brahman but still came to us as a master in Human form. Whatever He wanted His disciples and devotees to do, He Himself did and showed in a practical manner. There were eight principles of Sri Mahaprabhuji's teachings. Today I will throw light on just a few.

Sri Mahaprabhuji renewed the fire ceremony which prevailed in ancient times. He demonstrated how to perform it and gave it to us in a very simple form, since it had disappeared with the passage of time.

Before the creation of this universe, Brahma, Vishnu and Maheshwara (that is Shiva) used to perform yagnas to the Divine Mother. The Divine Mother was pleased by this and gave them each a boon: Brahma was to create the universe, Vishnu was to preserve it and Shiva to destroy it. That is why it is said that the fire ceremony is like the support of the earth.

How could Sri Mahaprabhuji give a boon to the world without performing yagnas? This is why He showed us how to do it.

The fire ceremony, or yagna, is based on scientific principles. In the fire ceremony, when you give an offering to a particular deity, it reaches that particular deity in its totality. In the Vedas it is written that the mouth of the Gods is fire—"agni." To whichever God you are giving the offering, by saying the mantra and adding the name of that God plus the word 'svaha' makes the offering complete; that is, you reach that particular God. The wife of 'Agni,' the lord fire, is 'svaha.'

To give a simple example: when you want to send money to someone in another place, you fill in a money order form and with that money order form you mention the name and address of the person who is to receive the money. Then you go to the post office; you are charged the money and get a receipt after which the entire responsibility of how to send it, where to send it, whom to send it to, is with the post office; it's no longer your business.

That is why our only duty is to chant the mantra with faith, devotion and the proper pronunciation. Take the name of the God to whom we are offering this ahuti, this offering, and then give it to the fire.

The law of nature, or life, is to give and take, as a farmer will sow a seed of rice in his field. He sows one seed but in return he gets much more than what he has sown. No computer can give you an account of how many billions of times it has given you more in return than what you sowed. That one grain of rice which you had sown, until such time as it doesn't go bad, will continue to give you tons and tons of rice—unless it goes bad—for when it goes bad, naturally, it can't produce anymore.

And it would be indeed very selfish of us, that, when the Divine gives us so much food, so much grain to pacify our hunger, gives us water to quench our thirst, we just keep on eating and drinking. But it is absolutely justified that when the Divine is giving so much, we should in return offer something back to the Divine and not just keep on eating it for our selfish pleasure. That's why we offer to the fire: when we receive so much grain to pacify the fires of hunger in our stomach, we should first offer of whatever we are earning, of whatever we are receiving, a little offering to the fire to pacify it and also give a little food or offering to those people who are hungry, to pacify the fire of their hunger.

And that's why it is said that a person who doesn't offer anything to the fire in a yagna or to the hungry people, just keeps on eating for himself, he is eating his meal in a very sinful way because he is only concerned with his own selfish hunger, with his own self. That's why he or she can never reach the spiritual heights of the purity of soul.

(Sri Shastriji has just recited this Vedic mantra which says that the person who cooks for himself or herself is a sinner because he or she does not share it with anyone.) Sri Mahaprabhuji showed this to us as long as He was with us in His physical body: He never took leave from the fire ceremony, every day He performed a yagna. Besides His daily yagnas, Sri Mahaprabhuji performed 171 very big yagnas in which hundreds of thousands of people came. He spent millions of rupees just on the fire ceremony and feeding poor people. Just as He performed the fire ceremony, the same way He satisfied the fire of people's hunger and all of you, or many of you, have witnessed that in Haidakhan every day many people—20, 50, 100—were fed by Him: He pacified the fires of their hunger.

Sri Mahaprabhuji gave us the practical example: when He Himself, the Divine, performed the yagna and gave food to the poor people, this meant that you common men should follow my example, because by doing so, by giving food to the poor, to the hungry, by performing yagnas, you are doing good to your own soul. It is an act to obtain happiness, bliss and peace in life, so follow the example.

There are many instances in the cultural history of India, of great kings of the past, Ambrish Nabhak, etc., of kings who performed yagnas, who gave away their whole kingdoms, their prosperity, their money, everything they had, using it up for doing these yagnas, until eventually one of them had just one earthen pot left. He had given everything to the fire (I mean he used up everything to pay the expenses of the fire ceremonies). He lived in the jungle just with an earthen bowl. Once a rishi came to him, asking him for something and the king said, "Your holiness, take this pot, for this is all I have and I am offering it to you."

Sometimes it happens that a child, when it is born, becomes the owner of millions and millions of rupees (or francs); he has acres and acres of land, he has everything that man could ask for—this is his destiny, while at the same time, another child is born who has no father, the mother is poor, so that the child doesn't even have the means to be given even milk, or any food, and his only sustenance is the name of the Lord. He can only repeat 'Rama, Rama.' This is the destiny of two children, born at the same time.

The one who has been blessed with all the prosperity, all the wealth of the world is the one who, in his past incarnation, had fed the needy, who had done the yagnas, and the result of his good deeds was that he got everything when he was born; he was born with a silver spoon in his mouth.

And the other one who was born in the poor house, where he had to strive for even a grain of food, was the one who in his previous life had not done anything to collect any good deed, any good karma; that's why he was given nothing, though the same Divine had created these two children.

It is written in the Vedas that when you meet a person, you can immediately know what this person's past karmas have been, because through the way he or she is born and through the way they live, it is obvious what their karmas were.

Sri Mahaprabhuji knew therefore the root cause to give happiness to mankind and that's why he started pleasing the gods first for the benefit of mankind by doing yagnas. We all have seen the result of what Sri Mahaprabhuji did: before He appeared, India always had to beg the United States for food grains. We were always the beggars and they were always the givers. They kept on giving us millions of tons of food every year. After Sri Mahaprabhuji appeared and had started perfoming yagnas, India had a grain revolution. Now the same land is growing so much food that we have bumper crops. Now there is so much grain in stock that the government doesn't have enough places to stock it. We certainly don't have to ask any other country for more grain.

As long as one can afford it one should always perform both kinds of yagnas: the first yagna is to feed humans, the second to feed the fire. I could tell you much more about this first principle but as there is little time, I will come to the second principle.

(Sri Shastriji is now discussing the second principle that is Sri Mahaprabhuji's ritual of giving chandan.)

In India, our forefathers always put chandan on their foreheads every day, but the same Indian people, in present times, behave very differently; for instance, we have a custom that when a son-in-law comes to marry the daughter, the mother-in-law, on receiving him, puts a tika, a sign, on his forehead, and then gives the bride away. Then the groom, the moment he left the house, would take out his handkerchief and wipe the tika from his forehead.

When Sri Mahaprabhuji started the ritual of applying chandan, the same people of India, barristers, lawyers, doctors, actors, all the fashionable people, used to queue up and vie with each other about who should be the first one to whom Sri Mahaprabhuju would apply chandan.

There is great importance in applying chandan, for it changes the lines of your destiny. Maybe most of you have heard or read about the famous story of Lord Krishna and his childhood friend Sudhama. The story goes that Lord Krishna—when he was a child and studying in Sandipani's ashram—had a brahmin friend who was from a very poor family. His name was Sudhama. Both of them studied together and were great friends. Then, when they had finished their studies, Krishna came to mathura and became the king and Sudhama went back to his father's house, because he was a poor brahmin. With the passage of time his poverty became more and more acute. He had children and his wife kept on telling him that we are so poor that we don't have enough food or milk to give to our children. And they are suffering, we are all suffering, what is the use of you having a friend who is the king, who has got everything, why don't you go to him and ask for some help. And Sudhama, who was basically a very shy person, did not want to take advantage of his friendship with the king, so he kept on refusing to go. But his wife was desperate, and one day she literally forced her husband to go to Krishna and ask for help.

Sudhama was very badly dressed because he was so poor, he had all his clothes torn, he had not even sufficient clothes to put around his body. When he came, Krishna recognized that it was the poor brahmin who had studied with him in the rishi's Sandipani Ashram. As he was a brahmin, according to the custom, he called for a bowl of gold and some water and washed Sudhama's feet in a golden plate. After washing them, he took the water as prasad. And Krisha made Sudhama sit with him on his personal throne of kings, of the Kingdom of Dvarika. Then Lakshmi, who is the wife of Vishnu (in Krishna's incarnation, she was the queen Rukmini), said to Krishna: "Oh, my master, what is this, what is this irony of fate that you are the king of Dvarika and your friend is such a poor man brahmin, this is very bad." So Lord Krisha started laughing and said: "My Queen, why are you worried, it is the result of his karma." So the queen said; "My Lord, you are a divine being who can change the laws of karma." The queen kept on insisting and eventually Krishna relented and said: "Very well, bring chandan."

Like Sri Mahaprabhuji used to apply chandan on our foreheads, the same way, when Rukmini had brought the bowl of chandan, Krishna held the head of Sudhama and put chandan on his forehead.

146

Then Lord Krishna said: "Lakshmi-Rukmini, on his forehead is written 'KSHA-YA-SHRI' which means 'annihilation of prosperity,' that there is no prosperity on his forehead."

Lord Krishna continued, saying: "But when I applied chandan on his forehead, I wiped out KSHA-YA and the opposite appeared: 'YAK-SHA SHRI,' which means treasurer of the gods and treasure of the world bank . . ." So Sudhama became the master of all the banks' money.

When Sudhama came home, his mud hut had gone and instead he had a palace. So he prayed to the Lord, saying: "You were so kind and gracious that with your divine hands you took hold of my head and applied chandan, changing thus my destiny so that I have become the most prosperous man on earth." And this is the great importance of chandan. And that's why Sri Mahaprabhuji changed the destiny and luck of all of us, you, me and everyone, by putting chandan on our forehead, He changed the line of our destiny.

Every man and woman has the chandan lines on their foreheads, even without chandan. You have a look into the mirror: either you have the three lines like this ($\equiv$), or like this (|||). These are the lines of fortune written by destiny. Those people who really know about reading the future, they don't look at your palm, they don't look at your face, they don't need to look at your horoscope either. They just look at your forehead and the lines on it, and they can tell you what is your destiny, what is your future life.

I want to share with you the principles of Sri Mahaprabhuji, the knowledge of which He showered on me with His grace in the thirteen years and more days I spent with Him. I am an old man, but when Sri Mahaprabhuji has bestowed such grace on me and He has sent me to you in my old age, I would like to give you whatever I have got from Sri Mahaprabhuji through His grace. I want to share with you everything He told me with His infinite grace, for I should not be a selfish man and take all that grace with me. I want to give to the people in Jagdambe this world whatever I have received through Sri Mahaprabhuji by His infinite grace. He used always to distribute whatever we offered to Him, and He never kept anything for himself—immediately He used to give things away as prasad. The

same way this prasad which He gave me with His grace I want to
give and share with you all.

BHOLE BABA KI JAI
SADGURU BAGHAWAN SRI
   HAIDAKHANDI
KI JAI
PARAMGURU SRI MAHENDRA
   MAHARAJA KI JAI
MATA KI JAI
HAIDAKHANDESHWARI MATA
   KI JAI
JAI VISHWA
SRI MUNIRAJI MAHENDRA KI
   JAI
JAI MAHA MAYA KI JAI
BHOLE BABA KI JAI

MAY 8, 1985

With the Divine Grace of Sri Mahaprabhuji, I threw some light on
two principles of Sri Mahaprabhuji's teaching: chandan and the fire
ceremony, yagna. I shared with you in a very short manner whatever
had to be told.

Today I would like to speak to you about mundan and the mantra
"Haidiyakhandi."

Indian culture is deeply associated with the Vedic culture, and when
a child is born in an Indian home, till it dies, there are 16 stages of
consecration which are performed on him or her. And these 16 Vedic
sanskaras are not only part of Indian culture, for the Vedas are the
support of the whole of creation, of the world, of the universe, and
that is why these 16 stages of consecration are meant to be performed
on each and every living creature.

The origin of the Arian race is, as you all know, from Europe, but
they wanted to explore the world and that is why they started to go
outside of Europe. And with the passage of time they reached India,
more precisely the Himalayas. And there, in the Himalayas, they

discovered the holy rivers Yamuna and Ganga. Himalayan beauty enchanted them so much that, in the search of knowledge, they decided to settle down there. They became the great sages and the rishis of the Himalayas, but while they lived there, they kept contact with the people they had come from. They kept on coming and going between Europe and the Himalayas, and they kept up the contact. It is also a well-known fact that the origin of the Vedas and its criticism was from Europe. From Europe also we collected many things and took them to India. In this continuation of giving and taking the culture was preserved. The sages were very keen that the complete culture of the Arian race should be shared by the whole world and that it should become one. But in those days the coming and going was not so easy—as the aeroplanes did not exist then, and therefore because of these difficulties it was not possible to communicate the Vedic culture to the entire world. Yet everything still depends on the Vedic culture.

I mentioned the 16 sanskaras: of the 16 stages of consecration the first one is the stage of conception. When the child is conceived in the mother's womb, this is considered the first sanskara, and when the embryo is seven months old, there is another ceremony which is known as the simanta ceremony. When the child is born, and when the placenta is cut, this is considered the third one. And the fourth sanskara, the mundan sanskara, which is known as the jhaule sanskara, is performed in the sixth month. And this sanskara is necessary for every human being. Keeping this in mind, Sri Mahaprabhuji made it more or less obligatory in Haidakhan that everybody should have a mundan. Before the initiation is given, before the sacred thread is given, the mundan sanskara is necessary. At this point it was performed regularly.

In the Bhagavad Gita, Lord Krishna says to Arjuna that this human body is like the tree called pipul tree, the ashwata tree. I'm sure many of you who have visited Haidakhan have noticed that there are two ashwata trees near Sri Mahaprabhuji's kutir. When Lord Krishna compared the human body with the ashwata tree, he meant that the roots of the tree are up above, and the branches face down, that it is not perishable, and that body is the ashwata tree. The wishes and desires of a human being are the leaves of this tree. Those who know this human body to be like the ashwata tree are the real knowers of the Vedas. In the human body, the crown chakra (sahasrara) is the root of the body and from that root the small twigs are the hair. And any good gardener knows that when he wants to plant a healthy tree and wants that tree to be strong, he will dig a sizeable hole. Further, from that small tree he will try to cut away all the small unimportant roots and keep on adding fertilizers to make it stronger, so that when the tree grows, it turns out to be a really solid tree.

The same way like the twigs of the ashwata tree, if the master doesn't get the hair removed from the head, a man does not grow in his spiritual pursuit, because the sahasrara (crown chakra) is the root of spiritual knowledge. The direct touch of the guru's hand on the head gives you the initiation of the shaktipat with which the kundalini energy is awakened. But if the hair remains on the head's crown and the guru touches it, the energy of power does not reach the sahasrara properly. And another thing: in a human horoscope, Saturn always tries to stop the progress of spiritual life and it is believed that Saturn lives in the hair. Until the hair is removed, Saturn keeps on pestering and impeding progress and is not pacified. And the power of thought doesn't develop, either, as much as when you have mundan. I am sure you will have had the occasion to observe that in those places where mundan is not done, people's minds are not as developed as it is in many places where this ritual is being observed.

Bearing this Vedic culture in mind, Sri Mahaprabhuji had this ritual performed as a necessity for the spiritual growth of his disciples. And while He was here with His physical body, whenever anybody came and whenever he thought that a person needed it, Sri Mahaprabhuji ordered that His disciples went through the ritual of mundan. And with this ceremony the disturbing influence of Saturn was annihilated.

Now I will share with you the most secret aspect contained in the mantra "Haidiakhandi."

With the grace of Sri Mahendra Swamiji Maharaja, the book "Shri Sadashiva Charitamrit" was written and published in 1961. Within his lifetime, the criticism and interpretation of this book was also written, but was not published then. A short while after Sri Mahaprabhuji appeared in 1970, Sri Mahaprabhuji said to me: "In your house there is a written book ready, please bring it here." And when I brought this book, "Shri Sadashiva Charitamrita" to Him, Sri Mahaprabhuji heard it from my own mouth from the first chapter to the end. And after having listened to the whole book, Sri Mahaprabhuji commented: "This is perfect, this is what I wanted." Sri Mahaprabhuji wanted that all religions should be united and that there should be a book in which they were given a common base, a universal book.

And I requested Sri Mahaprabhuji: "Now that you have appeared before the world, you should give it some teaching on kriya yoga." For kriya yoga had not been given fully, so I wanted that Sri Mahaprabhuji should complete His teaching on it.

Sri Mahaprabhuji told me that now the time is not ripe for the world to know the secrets of kriya yoga. When the time comes, he would open the treasure of this knowledge and give it to the world. As you might have read in the "Autobiography of a Yogi," there is a mention of kriya yoga, and also in many other books like this. But there is no book in which there is a description of how kriya yoga should be done, or how it should be taught. Everyone was told to go to the master, to the guru, and find out what it was.

These disciples in search of masters kept on wandering here, there, everywhere, and then would find a master who whispered something into their ears, telling them that this is how kriya yoga is done. But in our Vedic literature and all other religious books, nothing is secret, everything is open for everyone to interpret as they wish.

After my repeated prayers to Sri Mahaprabhuji that He should tell me what I should write, He told me that I should compose a ninth chapter. For each chapter He would tell me what I should write. And whatever Sri Mahaprabhuji told me, I wrote: it was the complete description of kriya yoga in His presence. Many times He listened to what I had written. But when He had finished, I prayed to Sri Mahaprabhuji, saying: "It will be impossible for the present mankind to follow this kind of yoga, because today at this stage, human beings eat all kinds of food which is not pure (as are vegetables, ghee, etc.), I mean, all the kinds of chemical food, and this is why it is impossible for them to follow this deep and difficult yoga."

So when I protested to Sri Mahaprabhuji that nobody would be able to do this yoga of present mankind, Sri Mahaprabhuji laughed and said: "Shastriji, don't worry. This yoga will be followed by someone who will be born—there is no end to time, and there is no end to the universe—somewhere, a human being will be born who will understand it and do this yoga. Maybe one person only, maybe five persons, or maybe a few more will understand it and will be able to perform and live this yoga and this will be sufficient to make it available to mankind, for it should no longer remain secret."

At the same time, Sri Mahaprabhuji told me: "If you are satisfied, if it makes you happy, I will teach you to present mankind of this yuga (era), the yoga of 'Haidiyakhandi.' " And as I was writing this literature on Haidakhan Babaji (in the '50s), Sri Mahendra Maharaja one day came by car to my house and told me: "Shastriji, all this time, we have been writing on Haidakhan, on Haidakhan Baba, etc. But now I have been given the permission by Babaji to tell the world the meaning of the name of 'Haidiyakhandi.' " So when I prayed to Sri Mahendra that he should tell me the secret mystery of the name Haidiyakhandi, he said that at the moment it is all right to just explain what is Haidiyakhandi: Haidiyakhandi is the one who lives on the continent of Haidakhan. Just as we have the European continent, or America and Australia are known as continents, the same way in India in ancient times, the different regions were known as "continents," and so Mahendra Maharaja said that this was sufficient for the world to know, that Haidakhan is the continent of Haidakhan Baba who lives in this continent. And Sri Mahendra Maharaji also said to me (Shastriji): "I'm revealing to you only a very small portion of what Haidiyakhandi means, but when Babaji appears to you and the world, He Himself will reveal to you the whole mystery of this name."

And when Sri Mahaprabhuji told me that He could tell me the secrets of the mantra "Haidiyakhandi" immediately, I was reminded of what had happened with Mahendra Maharaja years ago, when he had told me that, when Sri Mahaprabhuji appears, He Himself will tell you the real meaning of Haidiyakhandi.

And while explaining the meaning of this great name, Prabhuji told me that, when the actions of yoga start in the body, they start first in the muladhara chakra, from below. But this "Haidiyakhandi yoga" is a very special yoga which starts from the sahasrara chakra, from the top. And one by one, from above downwards, it will pierce all the chakras. When I further questioned Him to explain to me more

152

precisely, Sri Mahaprabhuji told me that there are five syllables in "Hai-di-ya-khan-di": In the Sanskrit alphabet, each letter has a particular place in the body. "Hai" has a place in the throat. According to the rules of grammar, "ai" is mixed in "Hai" and pronounced from the talu—the throat. Each of the five syllables has a letter both pronounced from the throat and belonging to the topmost chakra, so that in reciting these five syllables constantly, one travels only in the uppermost chakras, purifying them. And this Haidiyakhandi yoga, which gives everything to a human being who follows it, is a yoga between throat and crown chakra and has no connection with any of the lower parts of the body: it rules all the chakras from the sahasrara, from the top. By constantly chanting the mantra "Haidiyakhandi" all the chakras of a human being are pierced—and he becomes the owner of all the siddhis—the great powers which are known as the ashta siddhis—the eight divine powers, and the nau nidhis—the ninefold divine blessings. And this is one of the most important points of this yoga which Mahaprabhuji showed to us.

And one day—every day I was reading the "Haidakhandi SaptaShati"—while reading the last stanzas, I came across a sloka which I noticed immediately, for it contained these words: "By chanting constantly and repeatedly My name, a man obtains all the siddhis—all the powers of yoga."

Then again, Sri Mahaprabhuji showed me another mystery: according to the grammatical rules, when you join two words, it becomes different. The same way Sri Mahaprabhuji explained that the one who resides in "Haidakhan" is "Haidiyakhandi." And according to the grammar of Panini, one of the most famous Indian grammarians of Vedic times, you have to add 'i' to the name, whenever you want to change a male gender into a female gender. Then you have the feminine gender, like 'Shiva': Shiva is the male gender and when you want to make it female, it becomes 'Shivani,' by adding 'i' to the last letter. Also: Yam-Yami, Indra-Indrani, the same way: Haidiyakhandi. On this earth, there is not a single name in which, as it stands, has the male and female joined into one. Like 'Sita' is the female and 'Ram' is the male. They are two different names, but they become one by joining them, but they are two different names. 'Sita' is the shakti, the energy, and 'Ram' is the brahma. 'Radha' is the energy, "Krishna" is the brahma. That is why the one who resides in Haidakhan is called 'Haidakhandi,' that is the masculine energy. Then, who is the female energy? It is the queen, Mahamaya—Haidikhandi, the female energy, she is also part of this name—Haidakhandeshvari.

Many people offered prayers and did aarati to Sri Mahaprabhuji as Sri Mahaprabhuji. But there were times when people put a sari on Sri Mahaprabhuji, worshipping Him, offering aarati to Him as Mahamaya. And He proved it to us, that within Himself, Brahma and Mahamaya, both resided together. He proved to us that there is no need for us to do a separate sadhana, separate yoga for the male and the female energy, for Brahma and Mahamaya. By chanting, or doing japa of 'Haidiyakhandi,' we worship both together. For the universal good of mankind, Sri Mahaprabhuji has given us the great boon of this mantra. And when I finished the ninth chapter, I closed the book, so Sri Mahaprabhuji asked me: "You have finished?" So I told Sri Mahaprabhuji: "Yes, I have finished writing this book." So Sri Mahaprabhuji laughed and he said: "Well, now that the book is finished, and all is written down, what is the need for me to be here any more?"

BHOLE BABA KI JAI . . .
JAI VISHWA!

MAY 9, 1985

Sri Shastriji says that today he has been instructed to speak to you about fasting and worship. The subject of worship is a very vast one, and the whole of the Vedas deal with worship and in it; there is one whole chapter on this subject alone.

It is a great fortune for a man to be able to do worship. To be able to do puja, worship, is the greatest sadhana in life. The human body is, as you all know, made up of the five elements: earth, sky, water, ether and wind. The human body is created of these five elements and it returns (dissolves again into) these five elements. The whole of this complete universe too, is composed of these five elements, and when it is destroyed, it dissolves again into the same five elements. It is by the divine grace alone that a human body is created out of these five elements, and life enters into it with the divine grace alone. And as this body is made out of these five elements, consciousness is contained in it and is composed also of five organs. Actually there are nine organs, but five of them are considered the most important ones. And in this beautiful universe, they are interconnected through these elements.

And we have indeed been very fortunate to have the darshan of this most beautiful ashram. And the man responsible for this beautiful creation, this ashram, is Sundar Baba, and he is worthy of worship and darshan. And this indeed is the grace of Sri Mahaprabhuji on Sundar Baba. The Ramayana of Valmiki was written thousands of years ago, and from it the Ramayana of Tulsidas was created. In both these Ramayanas, there is a whole chapter, each called "Sundar Khand." The meaning of "Sundar" in your language is: "beautiful." And in these Ramayanas the most beautiful parts are contained in the "Sundar Khand." (Sri Shastriji is reciting this sloka which means: "Who is beautiful?—the person who is beautiful is beautiful both outside and inside.") And it is a fact that he is a man like this, who is beautiful outside and inside. This is why Sri Bhole Baba inspired him to start this beautiful ashram on this beautiful mountain. This ashram is the ashram of Siddheshwari Mahamaya. And when the Divine Mother Herself is dwelling in this beautiful ashram, a question about Her worship arises.

As far as my knowledge goes, I don't think that in the near or even further neighbourhood there is any place of the Divine Mother's worship. Wherever the Divine Mother does not reside, there is no peace. So it is indeed a great fortune for all of us that the Divine Mother has chosen to come Herself and dwell here. I would like now to express my thoughts to you and all about how to worship Her.

As I mentioned before, this whole universe is made up of five elements, and there is nothing beyond it. So, with the same five elements, we can offer worship to the Divine Mother. The first element is Mother Earth. Yet, according to the process of creation, the first element is ether, the last element on earth. The definition of the element earth is: smell, fragrance. That is why the first step in worshipping the Divine Mother is that we offer flowers full of fragrance, because with Her grace, Mother Earth is producing beautiful fragrance, that is, flowers on earth. Now, a man might dedicate his whole life to create a flower, but even with total dedication, he cannot create a natural flower. And when the Divine Mother has given us this gift through Mother Earth, it is our duty that we offer Her her own creation—the flowers. This is why we offer beautiful flowers to Her as the first step in worship.

Furthermore, there are different types of worship. You may begin five times, then increase to 16 times, then 100 times, then 1000 times, then 100,000 times, and then millions of times, depending on your devotion, and on how to want to offer worship. First of all, you fold your hands and meditate on the Divine Mother to call Her. After that you offer Her a seat, an asan. And to give Her a seat, you take a flower and put it there. This becomes Her asana. Then you offer Her water five times. First, to wash Her feet. Second, you offer Her water with your hands. Third, you offer Her water to drink. Fourth, you give Her a bath, and fifth, you give Her water to please Her. Water, too, is the Divine Mother's grace, because in spite of man trying, he can't create even a single drop of drinking water.

We offer water these five times to show our gratitude, for it is Her grace alone that She has given us this element of water, and without water we would all have died of thirst. Then the third step is to show Her the light-element. This is why the aarati is being done. Why do we offer Her light? Because, when the Divine Mother is seated before us and we are like an atom in comparison to Her greatness, we offer Her light as a symbol that it might remove the curtain of the darkness of ignorance separating us from her, so that this speck of light might unite us with Her infinite light, so that we may become one with Her.

After that, the fourth step is the element of wind. With it, we try to touch Her, because the wind-element is considered the element of touch. You will have seen that the pujari always waves a piece of cloth before the murti, after the aarati—this is how it is symbolized that with each stroke we are touching every organ of the Divine Mother.

The last step is the bells and the mantras we sing, the aarati we sing, because word and sound belong to the element of ether and with it, we are in contact with ether. Apart from thse five main elements, there is nothing on this earth which we can offer to the Divine. This is why we prostrate before Her, telling Her: This body is created by You and I am offering my body back to You. This is the most basic principle of daily worship. By offering worship, one obtains complete mental satisfaction. To have mental satisfaction is the greatest gift to mankind. Brahma, the Divine Mother, has given us the power of touch. Touch gives us an immediate, direct experience. Touch communicates the most varied of experiences to man—this is the gift of the Divine, of the earth-element to mankind.

The sense of taste on our tongue has been given to man through the water-element. There are six kinds of taste. The tongue has been given this gift of taste from the Divine through the water-element. If, by any chance, the Divine Mother was to take back this sense of taste, even the most delicious food could not be experienced by us.

The third gift to us is through light. The light-element is given to us through our eyes. When we are seeing through our eyes, it is the Divine grace we are using. If this Divine grace was to be taken away from us, we would be totally blind, in darkness, and the most beautiful natural sight, cinema, or theatre, would become useless to us.

The sense of smell is given to us by the element of wind: with our nose we can smell the most delicious fragrances, all the perfumes, all the natural smells. If this gift was to be withdrawn, although the nose might be a very beautiful nose, it would be a most useless nose.

The ether-element has bestowed us the gift of hearing. If this gift was to be withdrawn, we could not hear the most divine music or even any sound. It would be futile to live without the sense of hearing. Indeed, there would be no sense even in living without the five senses, even with this divine gift of a body, made of bones, blood and different kinds of nerves. We need to show our gratitude to the Divine, for if we can't offer to it the worship of these five basic elements, we would really be the most useless creatures. And I have shown you the shortest and simplest form of worship of these five elements.

Apart from these five elements, there are five kinds of air in the body. The wind-element has given us power in the body to use our arms, to be able to walk, to sleep, to stretch, to breathe, etc.

Shastriji has recited a sloka which means that, with the first step we take, we pray to the Divine Mother: "You are my soul-element." When we pray to the Mother, we say that my intellect, my mind is the Parvati-element (= essence of the Divine Mother). And Prana, the breath, are my friends who are always with me. And this building around is my house in which I dwell, that is, the body. Oh, Divine Mother, I spend a lot of time, energy, money to protect, to maintain this body. This too, is worship of You. And when I go to sleep, it is just like being in samadhi. And when I move about, accept it that I'm going around You in pradakshina (= sacred circumambulation). All the sounds that come out from the mouth of human beings—and all creation sings Thy praise. Whatever I work, whatever action I perform, is worship of You, oh Divine Mother.

And when this kind of feeling will be constantly with you, then this is real knowledge, when the whole sloka (prayer) recited above will become a way of life for you, then your whole life will become an act of worship. And then, slowly, slowly, you will become detached from this material world and attached to the divine world.

This is why Sri Mahaprabhuji in Haidakhan has given us the practical example by telling us to do karma-yoga always. And when we were collecting stones, when we were collecting earth, when we were collecting wood from the forest, or when we were washing dishes, or when we were cooking, we were doing the worship of the Divine Mother, for every act of karma yoga that we did was to offer it to the Divine Mother. This is what Sri Mahaprabhuji always said and this is why He kept on emphasizing and shouting: "Do karma yoga!" for it was your offering to the Divine. Because with His omniscience, Sri Mahaprabhuji knew that when He had called His beloved principles from far-off lands, He wanted to teach them the basic element of the Divine.

This is why He stressed so much the need for karma- and japa yoga. Because in this Kali-Yuga, by doing karma yoga and japa yoga alone, one can achieve all the Divine powers (= siddhis). Keep on working, keep on doing your job, and at the same time, with your mind, or with your tongue, keep on chanting the name of the Divine. What people used to achieve through pranayama (= breathing yoga), meditation and other disciplines, with Sri Mahaprabhuji's grace, one can achieve in this age by doing karma yoga and japa yoga (reciting the Lord's name).

When you are repeating the mantra which has been given to you, you pierce the five chakras with the wind-element in your body. And while breathing and repeating the mantra, what you could have achieved by doing a lot of pranayama, you achieve by simply repeating the mantra: with the power of the mantra, through the normal breathing cycle, you pierce all the five chakras of prana, apana udana, vyana and samana (= forward breath, downward breath, ascending breath, diffusing breath, assimilating breath). And whatever there is in this whole universe, is also in the body of man. Whatever you want to search from within, the whole body will come before you. There is all knowledge in a child: if we want to make him a doctor, we start him by doing studies of biology, and other things which are needed to be a doctor; one day, as he grows up, he will certainly become a doctor. And if the parents want that same child to become an engineer, if right from childhood he is taught mathematics, etc., one day he will become an engineer. And if the parents decide that the child should become a lawyer or a barrister, by teaching him law, one day he will become a lawyer. And this proves that in the human body, all knowledge is hidden: whichever thing we want to be, if we search for it, we will be able to realize that thing. And if we want that child to be a pickpocket or a thief, if we put him into this environment, one day he will become the most expert pickpocket. This proves that all the good and bad qualities are within the body, and that whichever way we want the body to act, will be realized by it.

And the same way, all the gods, like Brahma, Vishnu, Maheshwar (= Shiva), the Mother, every deity is in this body. And when anybody goes to a master for initiation, the master, with his Divine knowledge, will look into the person's heart and will immediately know that in the past life, this human being had been a worshipper of this particular deity, of the Divine Mother, of Shiva, or Rama. According to the knowledge of whom he had been worshipping in his last life, his master will give him the mantra of that particular deity. If he had been a disciple of the Divine Mother, he will give him (or her) Shaktipat (= initiation into the energy of the Divine Mother). This is why, in the initial stage, one needs to be with a master. For after showing the disciple the right direction, he progresses on his own later on. This is why, in this Kali-yuga, karma-yoga and japa-yoga are considered the most important forms of yoga.

And for these two yogas, fasting is supplementary. To purify the elements in the body, to find oneself, to purify all five elements in the human body. It is necessary to fast at least one of seven days. If you are traveling a long distance with a car, after a particular mileage, one stops, and opens the bonnet of the car, and allows it to cool off. In the same way, if a human body is just being fed, fed, fed, there is definitely a danger that one day this body will suffer many diseases. And Sri Mahaprabhuji always used to advise people to fast on Monday, for Monday is considered to be the day of Shiva. At the same time, the chief deity of Monday is the moon, and the moon is supposed to be the chief deity of mind. And to those people who do not have a sufficient balance of the fire-element, He said to fast on Tuesdays.

Probably you are aware that there is a religion called "Jainism." In Jainism, fasting has been given so much importance that they say continuous fasting is the only way of reaching self-realization. In Islam also, one month in a year, in the month of Ramadan, for 30 days, a continuous fast is observed. But this kind of continuous fasting is not good for the human body. Because there is an immediate loss of energy, and other detrimental effects. That's why, if a man fasts once a week, once in seven days, it is much more healthy.

You must all have been terribly bored by listening to all these things, so I will tell you the last thing and finish it off.

Do not think that the worship of the Divine Mother Siddheshwari is a very common thing. Sri Mahaprabhuji has given you this most important Divine gift of being able to offer Her Divine worship. All of you will have heard the name of Shankaracharya (8th century A.D.). He was the one who established the advaita (= non-dual way of religion). In order to establish his theory that there is only *one* Brahma, one ultimate Absolute, One Supreme Being, he went to different places and held discussions with many wise people and philosophers and established his schools everywhere. On his way, while meeting all these wise men, wise teachers, he reached the extreme northern point of India, which is called Kashmir. And there he invited all the wise

160

philosophers and teachers to come and discuss with him that there is only One Absolute Brahma.

But it so happened that, after inviting all these people, Shankaracharya had a very bad attack of diarrhea, so that he was not even able to walk a single step. As he was in the forest he told the people who were with him to take him out from the small hut in which he lived under the nearby tree. He was miserable, and suffering very badly, when a very small girl appeared before him. It was the Divine Mother in the form of a young girl. She came and said: "Oh, Brahmachari (celibate), what is wrong with you, why are you so sad?" And he said: "I have become without energy." So the Divine Mother in the disguise of that little girl, started laughing and said: "Oh, young man, on one hand, you are destroying energy and on the other hand, you are trying to establish the belief that there is only one Brahma. How is it possible that you can give importance to Brahma and ignore the energy, Shakti?" When he heard these words, Shankaracharya immediately realized his ignorance, his mistake and he prostrated before this young child, saying: "Oh, Divine Mother, forgive me, I understand my mistake!"

Without Shakti, there is not shaktiman, that is masculine energy. Without Shakti, nothing exists in the universe. From that moment, Shankaracharya started to worship the Divine Mother. And it is indeed the duty of each of you to come here now and again and to offer worship to the Divine Mother. Because this Divine Mother is the one who is protecting us from everything, who is the one who gives us everything in the world. To this Divine Mother, you should offer your love, your devotion, worship, your work, everything that you can, you should offer Her and feel grateful that you are given the chance to live in this world, because it is Her grace. You should take this message and spread this message of the Divine Mother and Her worship to different parts of the world from wherever you come. Teach people the feeling behind this worship and establish at different places temples of the Divine Mother and feel worthy of offering Her worship. And you all have all the material things one can ask for. You have lovely buildings to live in, beautiful cars to go around in, good clothes to wear, everything the material world can offer, you have. But unfortunately, you only lack one thing: the peace of heart and mind. And to get that peace, you all run here, there and everywhere, looking for it: You will find it only in the place of the Divine Mother.

And this is why my request to you is this: whatever I have talked to you about today, try and understand it, meditate on it, think over it and make the most of it.

BHOLE BABA KI JAI!
JAI VISHWA!

MAY 10, 1985

Bhole Baba Ki Jai!

Ladies and gentlemen, and children! You all are indeed very fortunate to be sitting in the court of Lord Haidiyakhandi, listening to the stories of His divine lilas.

Today I am going to throw some light on the incidents, on the background of how Lord Haidiyakhandi took human form and came on this earth for the good of mankind. Lord Haidiyakhandi is the absolute Brahma. To describe how He came to earth in human form is beyond speech, beyond the intellect of man. Thousands and thousands of people had His darshan, but there were very few to whom He revealed Himself, and they were the fortunate ones witnessing some of the things that happened.

To bring Him into a physical form on this earth was due to the prayers of a great saint called Mahendra Maharaja. Sri Mahendra Maharaja was born in the province of Bihar in India, in a small town called Manka. At the age of six, when Sri Mahendra Maharaja was still a child, he suffered from an incurable disease and to save him from this disease, Lord Mahaprabhuji appeared before him. And in the child's pure heart, the image of that saint remained inscribed in his heart. As he grew up, he kept thinking and meditating on the image of this saint in his heart. When he was nine years old, one day—it was his birthday—his mother asked him to go to a sweetshop and buy some sweets. She gave him some money and when he went to the sweetshop, he saw the same saint whom he had seen when he was a six-year-old boy. The saint, who was Sri Mahaprabhuji, blessed

162

him and told him: "Son, here are some sweets for you, go home, today is your birthday. I give you my blessings." When Mahendra Maharaja came home and gave the money back to his mother and also the sweets, she was very surprised and asked: "Who paid for them?" He told her the story, that there was a saint who paid. She took the boy with her and went back to the sweetshop, looking for the saint, but he had already disappeared. From that day on, Mahendra Maharaja's heart was very sad, as he always missed the saint, longing to meet him again. Mahendra Maharaja studied his maternal grandfather's books, who was a very learned man—and received a lot of knowledge from reading. By the time he grew up, his intellect and consciousness had developed so much that whatever he had read once stayed with him indelibly, for he had a photographic memeory. After some time he was not happy in the house and so he left home. But he continued his studies always. And he received his Masters Degree from Bhagalpur University. Then he came to Northern India and started to walk from Northern India to the west coast of India, to a place called Mount Abu where there is a famous siddha pith, a sanctuary of the Divine Mother called Ambaji.

And in search of his master, whom he had met as a child, he kept on doing penance at Ambaji for 22 years, still always searching for his master. After 22 years of penance, the Divine Mother Amba appeared before him, manifesting before Mahendra Maharaji, telling him: "My child, the guru you are looking for you will find in the Kumaon region, the foothills of the Himalayas. Go there and you will find your master." Mahendra Maharaja started walking, crossing one mountain top after another, always looking for his guru. The whole day he used to walk and whatever he came to at night, there he paused to rest. After having walked for days, one day he came to a place called Shitlakhet. Night had fallen, and in this place there was a teashop whose owner was a man called Shiromani Patak. When he saw Mahendra Maharaja, he realized that this was a great saint, so he requested him that, since night had fallen, he should come to his house as a guest to spend the night there. But Mahendra Maharaja replied to Mr. Patak: "I will not come to your house, but rather show me a place where I can spend the night in meditation and remembrance of the Lord." Mr. Patak said to him: "Mahendra Maharaji, there is a beautiful place down the hill, on the other side of the mountain, which is called Siddhashram. Spend the night in my house and tomorrow morning I will send my servant to take you there. You can live there as long as you want to." When he came to Mr. Patak's house, he went and sat down in a place where the old Haidakhan Baba in His former incarnation used to come and sit. When Mr. Patak saw that Mahendra Maharaja was sitting in the same place as old Haidakhan Baba had been sitting, he fell down, prostrating at his feet, and started to cry. Quite overwhelmed, he said: "Mahendra Maharaja, I'm very happy and honored that today you are sitting in the same place as the old Babaji used to sit; all the memories are flooding back into my mind."

And he was so overwhelmed by this experience that Mr. Patak started narrating story after story about Herakhan Baba to Mahendra Maharaja about what a great divine being he was, and about all the things that had happened during his presence on earth. He brought out all the literature he had written and showed it to Mahendra Maharaja. The whole night both of them spent talking about Babaji, and in the morning Mahendra Maharaja said: "Please send somebody, or you come and take me to Siddhashram." And as they were talking, suddenly they saw a man coming down from the hills who shouted and said to Mahendra Maharaja: "I would have come most happily with you but I just saw the pujari of Siddhashram who will accompany you there. I will come later and bring the foodstuff with me."

Mahendra Maharaja and the pujari went and when they arrived there, Mahendra Maharaja was very happy to see a most beautiful and peaceful ashram, and there was a spring also next to the ashram. The pujari told him that, when old Haidakhan Baba first came to this ashram, there was no water there and because there was no water, they asked for some people who looked for water with a divining rod. But even with a lot of effort, they could find very little water. So one day, old Haidakhan Baba took a bowl of water with Him and went there. First He smelt the water bowl and then He just started to dig in the ground with His hands when a strong spring welled up, wide like an elephant's trunk, and now there is a constant flow of water.

Mahendra Maharaja went to this spring and took some water, drank it and then took a bath also. There is a nearby very old Divine Mother temple of Vaishnavi Devi where he offered worship. Mahendra Maharaja described all these incidents in his autobiography called "Anupam Kripa." After a while he started to meditate there, but he realized that his mind was not in the meditation and he was not comfortable there, so he stopped and then fell asleep. He dreamt that the Divine Mother Vaishnavi Devi appeared before him, saying: "My son, I am hungry." So Mahendra Maharaja replied: "Oh, Divine Mother, You are feeding the whole of creation. It is not You who is hungry but this child of Yours who has not touched any food for the last three days and that is why You have pangs of hunger."

When he woke up, he saw Mr. Patak coming with a man, bringing everything to prepare food. In a short while food was cooked and offered to the Divine Mother Vaishnavi Devi as prasad, and then they all ate. For two to three days Mahendra Maharaja was quite content to be there, but on the fourth day he thought: "To live like this is no good. If by tonight my Lord and guru, the Supreme Divine Being, does not appear before me, I'll end my life here." Around one o'clock at night he woke up, went out of the cottage, and when he saw the studded sky, he became even more depressed. So again he went inside the cottage and locked the door from inside. After a short while, when he looked up, he saw Sri Babaji standing in full human form before him. He offered his pranams at His lotus feet. Babaji said to him: "Brahmachari, what is it you want?" So Mahendra Maharaja replied: "Only your grace." So Babaji put His hand on his head and said: "What else do you want?" Mahendra Maharaja replied: "Oh Divine Master, the way I am seeing You before me, I want all humanity to have Your darshan. Come and make the world happy." To which Babaji replied: "Your desires will be fulfilled."

Then Mahendra Maharaja was in seventh heaven, ecstatic with joy and after some time, he left Siddhashram and went to Haldwani. In Haldwani he said to some people: "Now that the Lord is coming on this earth, I have to go and do some work. I have to prepare the ground for his arrival. I have to prepare some literature so that people will know about Him." After that he lived in Vrindaban for some time or in Lobhan. In Vrindaban he used to stand in the queue of the beggars, begging for food, moving here and there. At night he used to sleep on the roof of the Shiva temple in Vrindaban called "Gopesh-wara." And he kept on visiting one place after another on foot. But later on in life, he used to go also by cars and trains. Once he was visiting a place called Bandikui in Rajasthan. In Bandikui, my younger brother was living who was a District Magistrate. One day a lawyer friend of his told him that a great saint had come, so he should go and have his darshan. My mother had been suffering from paralysis for 22 years. Therefore my brother always used to go to these saints and ask for a cure and blessings for my mother, but nothing had helped so far. After my brother arrived at Mahendra Maharaja's place and had his darshan, he realized that he was a great saint as well as a great man with much knowledge. And my brother requested him to come to his house the next day. Mahendra Maharaja replied: "Yes, I'll see." The next day, early in the morning, Mahendra Maharaja came with one of his followers to my house.

My mother was totally bedridden and could not move at all. When Mahendra Maharaja blessed her, touching her, what did we see? The next moment, she sat up in bed by herself! My brother then requested: "Mahendra Maharaja, please cure her completely," but Mahendra Maharaja said: "That is enough. Whatever had to be done, as much as she could be cured, I have done." Mahendra Maharaja then talked to my father, asking him: "How many sons do you have?" Then he also asked about the family. My father replied: "I have two sons: my elder son I have taught Sanskrit, and this is my second son whom I have taught law and he is a magistrate. We are a brahmin family of a town called Alwar and our family is the family of the 'raga gurus' (teachers of princes, heredetary advisors of the royal family). They used to perform all priestly functions at the court." (Shastriji belongs to this family of princely advisors. His father told Mahendra Maharaja nowadays the maharajas were no more, so he worked and his son also worked and that was how they ran the family.)

After some time, Mahendra Maharaja wanted to leave for Vrindaban, so my father, my brother and some servants took him to the railway station. And as luck would have it, I came by the same train from Alwar (Rajgarh). As I stepped onto the platform, I was surprised to see my father, brother and servants with a bearded saint—obviously, the saints wear safron clothes, so I understood him to be a saint. I wondered who was this man and quickly went to offer my respects to my father who said: "Son, here is a great saint, bow to him." Without asking a single question, I fell at his feet to offer my pranams, but he just took me in his arms, embraced me and, calling me by my name, said: "Oh brother Vishnu, now I have met you!" So as the train started to move, my brother asked Mahendra Maharaja when he would see him again, to which he replied: "After one month, when you both will be together in one place, I will come and give you darshan." And exactly on the thirtieth day, my brother was transferred from Bandikui to our native town of Rajgarh where I used to live. After that, I had many experiences and witnessed more miracles with Mahendra Maharaja. One day I will share them with you; now I just want to speak to you of my first meeting with Mahendra Maharaja.

What has he not given me! One day in Rajgarh, Mahendra Maharaja just touched my head and from that moment onwards, I started composing poems in Sanskrit which is a very difficult thing to do—but they just started to flow through me. And he said: "Today is the eighth day of the new moon and the Divine Mother's grace is on you, so whatever you want to write, start writing." After that, whenever I would sit down to write, a kind of plate of written words used to appear before me, and I would just copy it and keep on writing. And within ten days I wrote my first book called "Sadguru Kusumanjali." I took this book and offered it to Mahendra Maharaja in Vrindaban. And when Mahendra Maharaja had read the book, he said: "I'm very happy. You have written like the great old master poets of India, like Kali Das and all the others. Your language is as good as theirs, if not better. You have written everything I wanted the world to know about my Lord Haidiyakhandi." Then he wrote a letter to Mr. Vora, a publisher in Bombay to publish this book immediately. And Mahendra Maharaja made one comment: "Son, your Sanskrit poems are beautiful, beyond fault, but your Hindi translation is not as good as it should be. I would like you to write in such a manner that, after 450 years, the world will say that 'yes, he was another Tulsidas.' "

After that I stopped writing in Sanskrit and concentrated on writing in Hindi. It just kept on flowing. Then, during the nine-day festival of the Divine Mother, Navratri, Mahendra Maharaja sent someone to call me to come to Vrindabar. And it was the night of the seventh day of the festival. When I went and offered him my pranams, he said: "Now the time has come when you can start writing poems in Hindi as well." So I requested him, saying: "Please, give me some outline for this book." And he turned and took a small photograph from the shelf and that photograph was of the old Haidakhan Baba and it was covered by garlands. So he removed the garlands and took that photo and gave it to me. He also gave me the garlands and said to me: "Now go back home and put this garland on your little daughter (whom he had named Saraswati). She will tell you what to write." Saraswati was then four years old. When I had arrived, as I was instructed by Mahendra Maharaja, I put the garlands on my four-year-old daughter Saraswati, and the moment I put the garlands on her neck—she could not walk, so I was carrying her—she felt for my pen. So I took it out and from that time outwards, my daughter would just come, draw all kinds of lines on the blank paper that was lying there. Every day she would draw all kinds of lines, straight, crossed, or anything on several sheets of paper and I would just fill up as many pages with beautiful poetry. And as I would come to the last page which she had marked and made her lines, she would come running from where she had been playing outside and say: "Give me the pen," and she would again draw more lines on five, ten pages, so I kept on writing. And the whole of my family was amazed at what was happening. This was the happiest period of my life because at that time, Mahendra Maharaja visited my house at least 40 times. And whenever he came, he would say, "Come on, write, finish it off quickly, because when Sri Mahaprabhuji comes, when will you find the time to write? Finish it as quickly as you can, don't be late!" And my brother, who was a great devotee of Mahendra Maharaja, used to come and visit Mahendra Maharaja every Saturday and then go back to his work. He said to Mahendra Maharaja: "You make my brother write all these pages but without the presence of the deity, how will people understand who He is? There should be a murti (statue) deity about whom you are writing."

Mahendra Maharaja instructed my brother to go to Jaipur and there, my brother got three statues made and brought them to Mahendra

Maharaja. Then the question arose where these murtis should be installed. A place called Kathgharia near Haldwani was selected and there a temple was built and the murti of old Haidakhan Baba was installed. According to the Christian calendar this was in 1958. And the night before the installation, thousands of people were there for this ceremony. A divine light was seen by all of them which had the form of Babaji. And these thousands of people, men, women, children, all saw this with their own eyes, going into ecstasy on seeing this manifestation of Babaji appearing before them. Mahendra Maharaja called out: "He is here, He is here! The eternal form of Lord Shiva, Lord Haidiyakhandi is here!"

In 1969 my brother died in Ganapur while he held the post of District Judge. I wrote a letter to Mahendra Maharaja saying that "your servant and devotee, my brother, has died and I am without any support now." My brother left his body on June 10, 1969, and my letter reached Mahendra Maharaja on June 23, 1969. When he read my letter, tears started streaming from his eyes and he said: "When such a good devotee of mine is no more, what am I doing living in this world?" And he left his body, and in 1970 Sri Mahaprabhuji appeared, and on February 25, 1971, He was brought to Vrindaban. And this date, February 25, is the 12th day after leaving His body (= Sri Mahaprabhuji ie. February 14, 1984). And for 13 years Sri Mahaprabhuji kept on giving darshan sitting on His asana in Vrindaban. He went and gave darshan in many places, but these were the two main places where He resided—Haidakhan and Vrindaban.

Mahendra Maharaja used to keep on praying to Sri Mahaprabhuji: "Oh Lord, please come on earth and be involved with us, because when you are not involved with us, you are beyond the human mind, beyond the human race, and if you come down to this earth and you are with us, you can lift us up."

Sri Mahaprabhuji performed thousands of small yagnas, but His great yagnas were 171 in number, in which thousands of people participated, ate the bandharas. Hundreds of quintals of offerings were given into the sacred fires. And who has the capacity to bring down the Divine Supreme Being, the Divine Supreme Brahma, from up there to this earth? The great tapasya and self-sacrifice of Mahendra Maharaja could do this! And for just a minute manifestation, or for

169

a minute realization of the Supreme Divine Being, great sages have spent life after life in penance, in prayer. But with the prayer of Mahendra Maharaja, Sri Mahaprabhuji was brought down to this earth and we had the privilege and grace to see Him day after day for 13 years! And when Sri Mahaprabhuji wanted to reveal Himself to someone, even though that person was very far away, He gave that person indications revealing Himself to him or her, but when He did not want to reveal Himself, even those who were very close and lived with Him for 24 hours did not see anythng. His sole purpose of coming was to give grace to mankind. And every day, as long as He was here on this earth, He spent all His time, all 24 hours, to propagate "Om Namaha Shivaya," karma yoga, and the fire-ceremony, as you all have witnessed when you visited Him. In between His teaching karma yoga, the fire ceremony and "Om Namaha Shivaya," Sri Mahaprabhuji often used to emphasize that very bad times were coming and that there would be a revolution. And to counteract this great revolution, that it might wipe us out, we should partake in the great spiritual revolution. And the only way of not being wiped out by this great revolution is to participate in the great spiritual revolution by repeating the great mantras, like "Om Namaha Shivaya," by doing puja—offering devotion and worship. These are the only three things which can save man from the catastrophe. Whenever Sri Mahaprabhuji used to come out of His rooms—many of you who were in Haidakhan will have heard this call: BE ALERT! BE PREPARED!

And as He has taught us—we must change our hearts for the better. Once the bad heart changes into a good heart, from individuals to nations, there will not be any war but peace among nations. And if mankind is to be saved, Sri Mahaprabhuji appeared before and had told us, it is possible, since He had come to give us blessing and showed us the path, then we must change our hearts, we must take part in the spiritual revolution. Only then can we be saved. Shastriji has just quoted Mahendra Maharaja who had written that by a change of heart, the face of the earth can be changed. The change of the heart can change kranti into shanti (kranti—Hindi word for revolution, shanti—Hindi word for peace). And as great scientists are working every minute of their waking hours to create nuclear and other weapons to destroy mankind, the same way you should be partaking

170

in this great effort of repeating "Om Namah Shivay" or any other great mantra that you want to recite, and with this force, change the course of annihilation into peace. For spiritual strength is much greater, thousands times greater than material might. Sri Mahaprabhuji appeared to us for the benefit of mankind, to give all the good mankind was lacking. He wanted harmony and for mankind to be one family, only that there should be no class or caste distinctions. He wanted all the world to live together in harmony. Every country, all nations should be brothers. There should be no distinctions between colours, black or white or yellow. Everybody in harmony, unitedly, enjoy this beautiful creation of the Lord. And as you all have gathered here and are doing this beautiful job in this most beautiful place, the same way, spread the message of Sri Mahaprabhuji, of truth, simplicity and love to the maximum amount of people, to all corners of the world and start gathering together in harmony, in peace, in love and truth and simplicity, to live in that manner and unite the world as one big family. And at the end of every speech, Sri Mahaprabhuji always used to say: "Be fearless and the moment that you become fearless, nothing on this earth can touch you, no catastrophe, no other adverse force can touch you!"

BHOLE BABA KI JAI!
JAI MAHA MAYA KI JAI!
JAI MAHAPRABHUJI KI JAI!
JAI VISHWA!

MAY 11, 1985

Shastriji answers questions.

Bhole Baba Ki Jai! To the people who are dwelling in Switzerland, ladies and gentlemen, I'm very happy to stand before you today.

For thousands and thousands of years, the soul comes and moves around this earth. Today we are all here, assembled and so many souls are here and nobody knows who was whose father, who was whose daughter, who was whose brother, since we have no awareness of that.

We keep on coming and keep on moving from one place to another, from one life to another, without knowledge of the past.

I don't know what the reason is that has brought me here from thousands of miles away, I came here. What the relation is I have with you all, or what the relation is you all have with each other, all who have come here. But there is definitely some mystery to it. It is the most divine grace of Lord Haidiyakhandi, and the Divine Mother Siddheshwari Devi. The grace of Sri Mahaprabhuji made it possible that I came here, and the most magnificent attraction of the Divine Mother brought me here. This is certain.

Indeed, coming here, I received great joy and happiness to see that in this world there are still people who are simple in their devotion and simple in their hearts. With that divine grace of Sri Mahaprabhuji, it was made possible that the hymn to the Divine Mother Haidakhandeshwari Devi was published and translated, due to the great effort Malti and Sheila put into translating it. It is not of little significance that this has happened, but is a great event that this hymn to the Divine Mother has been published, for once it reaches all people, it will drown them with the great mystic power that it has.

I would like to ask your forgiveness but would like to say that in spite of your being able to spend millions of francs or dollars or whatever you want to spend, you won't be able to produce a Milton or a Shakespeare here at this moment, if you wanted to. The same way, even if we spent millions of rupees, we would not be able to produce our great poets Tulsidas or Surdas today. In like manner it is only Sri Mahaprabhuji's divine grace that this old servant of His is before you today. When you will start reading this book, you will remember in your heart and in your mind: "Yes, we have seen the old man who has created this work," and you will also say: "This old man visited our country." And I can assure you of one thing: that if you read this book "Haidiyakhandi Sapta Sati" with concentrated mind, you will most certainly feel the presence of the Divine Mother before you. I'm not just saying this for the sake of saying it, and whatever I say is being recorded. It is my faith and my belief and my promise to you, that the Divine Mother will manifest Herself and reveal to you whatever She wants to tell you before you, if you have faith and if you read this book with devotion. And the time is coming when you will all feel the taste of the yoga of devotion.

It is a most auspicious occasion that I have been able to say a few words and express the feeling in my heart to you. Now I would like to throw some light on the way you all are doing kirtan with devotion.

You all have been singing with great devotion and love "Haidiyak-handi, Haidiyakhandi, Haidiyakhandi sata chita ananda bol." In this there is three times the repetition of "Haidiyakhandi." And to fill the metre of this "Haidiyakhandi, Haidiyakhandi, Haidiyakhandi bol," there are in the next lines exactly three words given to match them. The first one is that Haidiyakhandi is the Supreme Divine. The second one is that Haidiyakhandi is the divine consciousness, and the third one is that Haidiyakhandi has the form of joy, happiness; that is, it gives complete happiness.

And the second stanza is "Samba Sadashiva, Samba Sadashiva, Samba Sadashiva bol," related with the word "palaka" which means "the one who takes care, who looks after things, the Haidiyakhandi who looks after the whole world." The second word relates to "prer-aka." "Prerak" means "to inspire" which is the "Haidiyakhandi who inspires you to do something." And the third one is "jagapati." "Jagapati" means the "Lord of the whole universe, master of all the worlds." And what a kirtan full of devotion it is, how much feeling it expresses! Nothing is left out. So why should one go anywhere else to get anything, what will one get elsewhere?

The Lord Haidiyakhandi, Sri Mahaprabhuji, blesses you with His divine grace that you may all prosper, be happy, healthy, wealthy, wise, and lead a fulfilled life. May all your desires be fulfilled and may you get the blessings to be at His lotus feet always. You wanted to ask some questions, but I'm not a very learned man who knows everything, I'm just a humble servant at the Lord's feet. Yet I will try and give answers to the questions which have been sent to us; Sheela will read them to me, and then in short I will try to answer them.

The first question is: "How can I help nature and the dying trees without joining an organization?"

Nature and man, both are external, man that is the Universal Self. Whatever nature lacks, whatever are negative qualities nature has to suffer from, no man can remedy, only the Supreme Brahman (Self,

God) can take care of it. The only solution that could be given is that you should all pray to the Divine: "Please let there be the rainfall of your nectar." Only then could it be saved. It is only pollution that has occurred with man's progressing technology as the reason for all this destruction happening to nature.

Babaji has spoken of great changes on the earth: "Where there are mountains, there will be sea; where there is sea, mountains will rise. Will it be suddenly over the whole earth, and when will this be?"

This creation has been there since billions of years, so it will not disappear like a soap bubble. Even to break up a huge rock, it takes a lot of time. There are all kinds of changes that do occur on this earth, but there won't be any sudden changes at any time. There are three types of changes, of "pralaya." The first type is day by day change. These are changes that are happening already always. The second one is long-term effect pralaya (khanda pralaya). The changes of this could be happening due to earthquakes, for instance, and that is also happening in many places. The last one is mahapralaya—total dissolution of creation at the end of time. In the place where Sri Shastriji lives, in Rajasthan in Central India, this last type happened. Once, suddenly thousands of buildings just collapsed and all over the place there was just water and nothing else. So these kind of changes do occur, although we are not aware of them every day, but still they happen. For the great Divine Being, for the Universal Self, one day is equal to millions of years of our time. When we count ten thousand years, this is just one twinkle of an eye for the Divine Mother. When She blinks, it is equal to ten thousand years of our time. What Sri Mahaprabhuji predicted, if you try to interpret it according to your Swiss timing, you will certainly be mistaken. It won't happen, because what He spoke of was on a universal level: pralaya *will* happen, but it will take some time.

The third question is: "I read a book that says that the centre of the earth is being prepared as refuge for higher extra terrestial beings for the coming possible holocaust and that this will be for the people who are devoted to God and will so be prepared more fully for the New Age. Is this true?"

As we are on this earth, there are six other worlds (lokas) above us. The first one that is "bhu loka," the earth. Above that is "bhuva loka," the third one is "svaha loka," the fourth one is the "maha loka," then there is "gyana loka," and then the seventh, last one, is the "satya loka." Over all these seven worlds there is the world which has been imagined by the mind as "manashakti," the residing place of the Divine Mother, "manipura." So you must imagine that as on this earth, we are being governed by different governments and many programs, so many things are happening every moment, every day, year after year, the same way, in all the different worlds above us, every day, every moment something or the other is happening. And that is why in the Vedas, it is quoted that like the pores of your body, so in each pore of the Universal Self there are billions of universes. So what is this universe? It has a relative significance. The real form is the greatest of great Universal Selves is that in each pore of His skin, there are billions of universes.

The fourth question is: "Is there still, in a hidden place in the Himalayas, Babaji physically present? Can one go there and have His darshan?"

Sri Mahaprabhuji, Babaji, is not hidden in the Himalayas only. He is everywhere, all over the universe, in every atom as the Infinite Being, and it is your love and devotion which will make Him manifest before you any moment when your devotion and love will call for it. If there were to be one person amongst us like Mahendra Maharaja, Sri Mahaprabhuji would not be able to refrain from physically being with us. Is there anyone like that among us?

The fifth question is: "What is the significance of the trishul?"

The trident, or trishul, is the chief weapon of Lord Shiva. It has three points—this is why it is called the trident, or trishul. Lord Shiva uses this trishul, this trident, as a weapon for removing the three thorns which are in the hearts of His disciples. They are the spiritual thorn, and the second one is the thorn that has come accidentally from the Divine, and the third one is the thorn which has come to you by accident from nature. Shiva uses this trident to pick out this thorn from your body like you extract a thorn from a banana. The trishul is a weapon and is always in Lord Shiva's hands. Lord Shiva is considered the master of weaponry. There are two types of weapons: one is called "shastra," and one is called "astra." The trishul is a shastra, a weapon which you keep in your hands without letting it go from your hand. Astra is a weapon which is like a bullet, which comes from the rifle, destroying whatever you want to destroy. When you read Indian religious books, you will come to understand the meaning been given to things, that Lord Shiva is always shown moving with the trident in His hand, to protect His devotees from accidents with the three things we talked about, the spiritual thorn, nature's thorn, and the divine thorn. Further the three gunas (qualities), the "sattwa guna," the "raja guna," and the "tamas guna" are there since the creation of the worlds and Shiva uses the trishul to discipline nature with these gunas or qualities (= to restore its balance). With the trishul, the "damru" (drum) is always shown which we play during aarati. I'm sure you all have seen it and it is always tied to the trishul. Lord Shiva has used this damru to create language, the sounds of all the languages. From the damru comes the original sound, or sounds. And when Lord Shiva saw that the worlds, the universe was to be created, He also saw how it would be created. From ether came the word, for the word is sound. This was the first creation of the universe. It is said in the Vedas that when the universe was created, Lord Shiva started to dance, saying "Om Namaha Shivay . . . Om Namaha Shivay," and He danced the "tandava" dance. Lord Shiva repeated "Om Namaha Shivay" in His heart. When Lord Shiva played the damru, the word that came out was a Sanskrit word of 14 letters. What Shastriji just said, I can never say in seven lifetimes. These 14 letters (Shastriji will repeat them again) were what came out when Lord Shiva played the damru. And from these 14 letters, Panini, Katayayani and Patanjali created the 14 sutras and the whole grammar of all languages. And it is said that from these 14 letters the great grammar of the Sanskrit language would be created for mankind to use in all times to come.

The sixth question is: "What is the significance of chandan and its colours?"

In chandan, the yellow colour gives prosperity, it increases prosperity. And the red spot made in the centre, on the "ajna" chakra, is the seat of the Divine Mother and is being put there to give protection to that chakra. And the rice that is placed on the red spot is to give satisfaction to the soul. Many times you put the rice but it will fall off. Somewhere you can't stop it and are not even aware of where it has fallen. It is the greatest sacrifice of its kind. About this there is a story: One day Parvatiji, Lord Shiva's wife, applied chandan and then put the red spot (kumkum) on it and then rice. Lord Shiva and His wife then went for a long, long drive, and when they came back again, the box with chandan, kumkum and rice in it was opened. To that box however there was now an end which is life's end. And Lord Shiva said to Parvatiji: "Before this end was put into this box, food was already supplied to it, to keep it alive. In the same way the Lord provides milk for a child before the child is born, whether it's a human child, or an animal, to keep it alive, the Lord gives milk into the mother's breast and for the animals it is the same." Secondly, Lord Shiva is also the Lord of food. Sri Shastriji just recited this mantra from the Yayur Veda, in which it is written that every grain of food has the element of the Divine, the Absolute Self (Brahman) in it, because it gives life.

The seventh question is: "How do the mantras work on the body: Om Namaha Shivaya, Om Haidiyakhandi, and Om Hrim Shrim Haidakhandeshwaryai Namaha!"

I have mentioned before that whatever is outside in the universe, is also in the body. The same way, there is a place for each deity in the human body. It has its place there, like Lord Shiva, like Lord Haidiyakhandi, Brahma, Vishnu, Mahesh, the Divine Mother, Isamasai = Jesus Christ, all the divine beings, all the gods have a place, a seat in the human body. And the maker of this body has also given keys to these different places and these keys have different numbers—the mantras, to open the places with these keys, so as to reach that particular God. Sri Shastriji says that these different letters and these different words have different ways of reaching different places of your body through all the channels of your veins, carried along by the five airs "vyana," "apana," "prana," "udana," "samana." And they pierce through with your breathing cycles, reaching the places that when you say a particular mantra like Krishna, Rama, Hrim, the sound for the Divine Mother. So every mantra, every letter has a way of getting collected through your breathing at one spot, piercing that spot and reaching the deity residing there. And by repeatedly repeating this mantra, this name, you create a sort of a collection of energy there, and the key fits the lock and the number of the lock opens. And the greatest of great yogis used to do this kriya, this work, to open the different chakras by repeating these mantras. But the sages of ancient times realized that by doing these different mantras to reach different gods, it will take a very, very long time. So they started experimenting with different letters, with different mantras, and they created many, many mantras, to see which was the quickest, fastest way to reach that spot—and it is the same way that we are trying to develop all the nuclear weapons: all the scientists of the world are concentrating on finding out how to create the most expedient weapon. The same way these mantras can act. Om Haidiyakhandi (three times) is the ultimate Divine Mother, the great knowledge and mistress of all the ten great types of knowledge. In this world there are different kinds of religions, different kinds of people and they all believe in God in different aspects, by different names, but the Divine Mother the whole world acknowledges, and Her worship is offered with the same kind of ritual everywhere. And you will ask how and why?

You will see in the early morning all the young children, girls and boys, will all collect their books and get ready to go to school. And when it is office-time, all the doctors, judges, all the lawyers, and all the businessmen will pick up their files and go to their offices. And this identical system exists in Russia, America, India, Switzerland, Japan, everywhere. And this is the worship of the Divine Mother Saraswati who is the chief giver of all knowledge. She is the mistress of knowledge. And whether it is in India, Russia or any other part of the world, all the children, the elders, in order to gain knowledge, have to to their place of work with their books, they have to pray to the Divine Mother called Saraswati. And the world over, all businessmen go to their factories, their offices, their shops, or wherever, they all worship the Goddess Lakshmi, the Goddess of money. And the world over, all businessmen have the same attitude, that when a customer comes, he is talking to a customer, I mean explaining everything to him, but in his mind he has this one thought: "The sooner I sell him my goods and the sooner I get his money into my pocket, the better it is." This is the same everywhere, a kind of sadhana, like the yogis who are sitting and waiting, doing their sadhana to reach Brahma, the same way a businessman is sitting at his place of work from morning till evening, trying to get your money into his pocket.

This is the worship of Mahalakshmi, the Goddess of prosperity. All the armies in the world, every defense budget, is being established to create new weapons, and all armies are doing their marching "left-right-left-right" every day without fail, and they are guarding all the borders, and you will see the soldiers trying out new weapons, new guns, new tanks, new aeroplanes are being flown and new atom bombs and nuclear weapons are being created every day, the world over. Isn't this the sadhana of Mahakali, the Goddess of destruction? And all the world over, each and every human being, in some form or other, does a sadhana, offering worship to the Divine Mother, Saraswati, the Goddess of knowledge, Mahalakshmi, the Goddess of prosperity, and Mahakali, the Goddess of destruction. There is no exception in this anywhere. The only difference is how and where, in which manner you offer your worship. There are different forms and different rituals, that's all, but otherwise the whole world is offering, worshipping that divine energy of Paramba, the great Divine Mother.

The eighth question is: "What is kriya yoga? I want to learn it."

What Sri Mahaprabhuji said about kriya yoga is being translated into English by Srimati Malti Devi, and very soon this book will be published and you can read it and find out what kriya yoga is. It is a big book of 1300 pages and it will take a little longer than Haidikhandi Sapta Shati to translate, but it will be ready very soon.

The ninth question is: "What is mansa yoga? It was taught by Mahendra Maharaja and why does it not get emphasized?"

This, Sri Mahaprabhuji with His own divine lips has explained also in the same book which is being translated by Malti. And I'm indeed grateful to you all for listening to me all these days with such concentration, and accepting whatever I said in my broken language and giving me so much love and attention. I would like to express my gratitude to you and give you this, that you may prosper, may you always remain with your devotion in the presence of Lord Sri Mahaprabhuji.

BHOLE BABA KI JAI!
JAI MAHA MAYA KI JAI!
JAI VISHWA!

179

Sundar Singh speaking:

I would like to thank Shastriji for the very great teaching he has given us during these afternoons. I feel that his knowledge is just endless and we are getting the deepest truth. I also feel that I found a teacher as never before in my life in these few days and I want to thank him so much for that.

For information: Contact Sundar Singh (with his family pictured above) at: SCHWEIBENNALP, Chalet Zimmer Massenlager, 3855 Brienz, Switzerland, (036 513289).

For information on going to India in my group, contact Ramloti, (719) 256-4108.

CHAPTER 13
CLOSING

Finding the Australia Within You

I wrote this book in Australia, a country I love dearly. Of course each country of the world has a special place in my heart, and each brings me something unique. Now I bring you the energy of Australia.

A Japanese teacher once said, "India is the roots, China is the trunk, Japan is the branches and trees, and Australia is the fruit." Maharishi, founder of the Transcendental Meditation Movement, has said that Australia will be the first country to get totally enlightened in the New Age. And many other people say that Australia is the "future." Of course, anywhere *could* be the future at any time, but it behooves us to consider what is going on in Australia at this time—and incorporate that energy now.

Australia is a beautiful, self-supporting country that, among other things, can boast the presence of Ayer's Rock—the largest rock in the world. But it is no ordinary rock, not by any means. It is a rock made of iron—a magnet—a power chakra and major spiritual center that is sometimes called the "Solar Plexus of the Earth." Recently, Ayer's Rock was ceded back to the Australian Aborigines.

Now, in considering Australia and its spiritual energies, we have to think about the Aborigines—the oldest surviving "race" or "culture" of humans on earth, having been around for something like 75,000 years! I am in awe of the fact that the Aborigines had a natural spiritual purification of their own through "fire ecology." They

183

consciously started bush fires for the purpose of regeneration. (Babaji has spoken often about the importance of this type of purification by fire.)

Along with this ancient culture, Australia also encompasses such newness, such aliveness right *now*. It's a unique spirit—a freedom from tension, a willingness to enjoy the moment, to party, to have fun now. When I was considering a retreat to work on this book, I discussed the many possible locations with a Kahuna from Hawaii. Australia became the obvious choice. I was already heading in that direction on a tour. Why not go two weeks early to some remote spot? In a flash it was decided. And one telephone call later I was offered a resort house two-and-a-half hours from Melbourne, in the little beach town of Sorrento. Since the resort hose was owned by Anne Le Souef, the Center Manager of the Melbourne LRT at the time, I felt right at home.

Being there reminded me of my hometown. I grew up in Grafton, Iowa—population of 300. There, people were warm, sincere, simple, and wonderful.

Since I was there to "retreat," I spent a great deal of my time fasting and remaining in solitude. For the first week I did nothing but my devotions—chanting, meditation, studying *A Course in Miracles*, rebirthing, and doing Ho'O'Pono Pono. I had no book in mind when I went there, though I knew that one was "coming." I was about to "conceive." I decided not to control the situation. I tried to be completely open. Usually, I have a book in mind that I want to write, often with the outline completely done before I go into solitude, but in Australia, it wasn't like that. This time was different. I was trying to surrender to God more, to the moment, to the energy there.

I asked my teacher, Babaji, to guide me.

In one meditation, I heard the instruction, "You must teach people to love God more."

"What a great assignment!" I thought.

"Well, then, what is the title?" I asked.

Then I heard the words: *Pure Joy*. And I was thrilled.

So I began to work, and after ten days, I knew I was on the right track because Babaji paid me a visit one night on the astral plane—I was suddenly "going to India." I was flabbergasted, because I had actually visited India twice just the year before. I couldn't believe that I was going back so soon. Then, suddenly I was there, and there he was. He called me up to him in front of a large group of people and told me to sit next to him. I was very startled to see that he had a ball of fire in his left hand, coming right out of his palm. When I sat down next to him, he placed the fire on the ground.

I probably wouldn't have remembered this experience on the astral plane, except that just as it was happening, I was startled into waking consciousness by a loud crashing on the roof. It sounded as if trees were falling onto the cottage. I sat straight up in bed and realized that there were no trees falling. And then I knew that Babaji had awakened me with this "noise"—so that I would remember the astral plane experience with complete and vivid recall. I felt as if I'd had a "fire purification." I was in an altered state. My body cleared. I was very inspired to continue writing and was flooded with enthusiasm and creative energy.

There is a "light" in Australia that can not be denied or extinguished. There is a real willingness to "go for it!" I have been very impressed with the rapid success of the Loving Relationships Training there. I truly acknowledge Vince and Yve Betar (who are now trainers of the LRT) for opening the Melbourne Center and for successfully passing it on to Jennifer Blackie and Anne Le Souef, and I acknowledge all the graduates who have chosen to share the message of the LRT in their country. I acknowledge all those who helped start the Sydney Center also.

There's an attitude in Australia that I really like. The people there will use the phrase, "No worries, mate," which means *no problem, it's handled*. Another saying is, "She'll be right!"—which means that everything will be okay. Other phrases include: "Fair Dinkum," which means *True*; "For Real," or "Ultimate Truth . . . sealed," which are both common comments and greetings.

Australia is booming. There is a tremendous amount of *space* (Australia has a land mass the size of the United States minus only the area of Washington state and the population of New York state), and there is so much air to breathe and everyone knows there is enough. There's a longing for the truth and a real response to the truth. There is an opportunity to purify oneself very quickly in Australia.

One of my psychic friends said to me that Australia has a "spleen energy"—an energy of encouragement, support, and enthusiasm. Let's incorporate that spirit again and again in ourselves, that spirit which is always available everywhere.

Prayers for the Closing of This Book

I accept the Atonement for myself
I place what I think under the guidance of the Holy Spirit
I commend my Spirit into the hands of the Father
I offer my faith to the Holy Spirit
I choose to be led by the Holy Spirit in Christ's Service
May the mind be in me that was also in Christ
I allow the Holy Spirit to undo all my wrong-thinking
I return my whole mind to God

Ending

"There is one thought in particular that should be remembered throughout the day. It is a thought of PURE JOY: a thought of peace, a thought of limitless release, limitless because all things are freed within."

—*A Course in Miracles,*
Teacher's Manual

RESOURCES

For ordering pictures of Babaji and tapes, write or call:

Haidakhandi Universal
Ashram
P.O. Box 9
Crestone, CO 81131
(719) 256-4108

The following bodyworkers are highly recommended. Their specialties are noted in parentheses after their names:

Don McFarland (Body Harmony)
1535 Sixth St. (103)
Santa Monica, CA 90401
(213) 393-6900

Patrick Collard (Body Thought
Release)
413 Ave Teresa
San Clemente, CA 92672

Kermit Stick (Rolfing)
3876 Bridgeway N.
Seattle, WA
(206) 547-8382

Dr. Michael Faila (Chiropractic)
1666 E. Olive
Seattle, WA
(206) 323-1666

Dr. Joe Adler (Chiropractic)
350 Central Park West
New York, NY 10025
(212) 749-7110

Terry Milligan (Past Life Work &
Adjustment)
P.O. Box 1924
Rohnert Park, CA 94927
(707) 792-0180

Recommended Reading

The Autobiography of a Yogi, by Pramahnsa Yogananda (Los Angeles, CA: Self Realization Fellowship, 1974).

Beyond Mortal Boundaries, by Annalee Skarin (Marina del Rey, CA: De Vorss & Co., 1972).

A Course in Miracles, (Tiburon, CA: Foundation for Inner Peace, 1975).

The Door of Everything, by Ruby Nelson (Marina del Rey, CA: De Vorss & Co., 1963).

From Here to Greater Happiness, by Joel M. Teutsch and Champion K. Teutsch (Los Angeles, CA: Price Stern Sloan, Inc., 1975).

The Life and Teachings of the Masters of the Far East, Volumes 1-5, by Baird T. Spalding (Marina del Rey, CA: De Vorss & Co., 1924-1955).

New Teachings for an Awakening Humanity, edited by Virginia Essene (Santa Clara, CA: S.E.E. Publishing Co., 1986).

Starseed Transmissions: An Extraterrestial Report, by Raphael (Kansas City, MO: UNI-SUN, 1983).

Vision, by Ken Carey (Walpole, NH: Stillpoint Publishing, 1986).

Ye Are Gods, by Annalee Skarin (Marina del Rey, CA: De Vorss & Co., 1973).

Books by Sondra Ray

Celebration of Breath (Berkeley, CA: Celestial Arts, 1983).

Drinking the Divine(Berkeley, CA: Celestial Arts, 1984).

I Deserve Love (Berkeley, CA: Celestial Arts, 1976).
Ideal Birth (Berkeley, CA: Celestial Arts, 1985).

Loving Relationships (Berkeley, CA: Celestial Arts, 1980).

The Only Diet There Is (Berkeley, CA: 1981).

Rebirthing in the New Age, co-authored with Leonard Orr (Berkeley, CA: Celestial Arts, 1983).

Books by Bob Mandel

Open Heart Therapy (Berkeley, CA: Celestial Arts, 1984).

Two Hearts Are Better Than One (Berkeley, CA: Celestial Arts, 1986).

Co-Authored by Sondra Ray and Bob Mandel

Birth and Relationships (Berkeley, CA: Celestial Arts, 1987).

The Loving Relationships Training

The Loving Relationships Training (LRT) is produced by Guided Productions, Inc. By using this name we recognize that our job is to serve a higher purpose and to be guided by something bigger than ourselves. At this time, there are four partners in Guided Productions—Bob Mandel, Mallie Mandel, Fredric Lehrman, and myself.

For information on the *Loving Relationships Training*, please call us at our toll-free number: **1-800-INTL-LRT (1-800-468-5578)**.